Presented to

Dorothy Melling

By

Kevin & Martha Melling

On the Occasion of

Christmas

Date

_2005_

My Heart

WILL GO ON SINGING

My Heart
WILL GO ON SINGING

REDEEMING THE GOLDEN YEARS
FOR THE GLORY OF GOD

N. A. WOYCHUK, M.A., Th.D.

BARBOUR
PUBLISHING, INC.
Uhrichsville, Ohio

All Scripture quotations, unless otherwise noted, are taken from the New King James Version of the Bible. Copyright ©1979, 1980, 1982 by Thomas Nelson, Inc. Used by permission. All rights reserved.

Scripture quotations marked KJV are taken from the King James Version of the Bible.

Scripture quotations marked NASB are taken from the New American Standard Bible, ©1960, 1962, 1963, 1968, 1971, 1972, 1973, 1975, 1977 by The Lockman Foundation. Used by permission.

Published by Barbour Publishing, Inc., P.O. Box 719, Uhrichsville, Ohio 44683 http://www.barbourbooks.com

ecpa Member of the
Evangelical Christian
Publishers Association

Printed in the United States of America.

Contents

Until Then. 11

Greet the Unseen with a Cheer! 12

Do Not Count the Years. 15

Grow Old Along with Me 17

Me, Myself, and My Tomorrows 19

The Vintage of the Western Slopes 24

I've Only Begun to Live 26

Not Knowing. 28

I Will Hope Continually. 30

How Firm a Foundation. 31

Sweet to Reflect 34

And Still Growing 36

Age Is Opportunity. 39

Inward Peace and Inward Might 40

Communion with God. 42

The Happy Soul. 44

The Ages Come and Go 46

With Thee Is Rest. 48

I Know! 50

A Prayer. 53

The Lord Will Provide 56

Can You Remember 58

Unpremeditated Art 60

Today. 64
Let God Plan for You 65
The Path I Have Prepared for You. 68
If We Could See Beyond Today. 70
Some Time We'll Understand 72
Let the Beauty of the Lord Our God
     Be upon Us 75
Rest. 77
Trusting in My Father's
     Wise Bestowment 79
If My Days Were Untroubled 81
Think Through Me Thoughts of God. . 84
He Maketh No Mistake 85
A Heart at Leisure from Itself 87
Re-Ignited 89
Not Time Enough 91
The West Winds Blow 92
Delighting in the Word of the Lord . . . 95
Delight in God Only 103
Let Me Get Home Before Dark. 108
Sometimes a Light Surprises 112
Recalling His Mercies. 114
We Should Remember 116
They Also Serve 118
I'll Trust in Thee. 120

The Light of the Spiritual Life. 123
I Wish You. 125
God Knows 126
It Is a Beauteous Evening 128
The Secret Things. 130
Called. . .Held. . .Kept 132
Content and Discontent. 133
Liberty of Heart. 135
Peace Is the Pillow for My Head 137
Contentment 139
The Ancient One. 141
Human Argument at Its Best 165
The Sands of Time Are Sinking 172
It Lies Around Us like a Cloud 175
A Psalm About the Shortness of Life . . 177
My Heart Leaps Up 179
Joy Shall Overtake Us. 180
No Wrinkles in My Soul. 182
An "Envelope"—the Immediate Body . 184
Joy, Shipmate, Joy. 188
The Story of a Dream. 191
We Shall Be like Him. 197
It Grows More Real Day by Day. 199
Thanks. 201
The Way In 203

Beyond the Sunset 207
Our Ultimate Perfection 209
Death Itself Shall Die 211
How Long the Night 213
The City of Celestial Health 216
Clothed with Immortality 218
What Is This Splendor? 220
The Setting Sun 223
Mourn Not the Vanished Years 225
The Day Just Begun 228
Remembered Joy 230
Glory Beyond Words 232
Sunset and Evening Star 236
On the "Elegy Written in a Country
    Churchyard" 238
The Elegy 240
The Epitaph 250
Acknowledgements 252

UNTIL THEN

Then I, John, saw the holy city.
REVELATION 21:2

My heart can sing when I
    pause to remember
A heartache here is but a stepping stone—
Along a trail that's winding always
    upwards—
This troubled world is not my final Home.
But until then, my heart will go on singing;
Until then with joy I'll carry on—
Until the day my eyes behold the city
Until the day God calls me Home.

STUART HAMBLEN[1]

GREET THE UNSEEN
WITH A CHEER!

General Douglas MacArthur on his seventy-fifth birthday recalled appropriately the lines written by Essa Lott when she was ninety years old, "We are as young as our faith and as old as our fear." Let that faith rest upon what God has told us in His word, and we may heartily sing Toplady's lines:

Sweet to look back, and see my name
    In life's fair book set down;
Sweet to look forward and behold
    Eternal joys my own.

Sweet to reflect, how grace divine
    My sins on Jesus laid;

Sweet to remember that His blood
My debt of sufferings paid.

We mourn not the vanished years, as the west winds blow, but with the April rain of smiles and tears, our hearts are young again. We listen to the profuse strains of unpremeditated art sung by the soaring bird; we observe the lilies how they grow—how *peacefully* they grow, how *trustfully* they grow, how *royally* they grow, how *exemplary* they grow; the birds and the flowers are but teaching us how to sing and how to grow in the blessed care of our heavenly Father.

So in awe and delight, and with the "spills" of glory of sea and sky and the mystery of the purple hills, we go on without knowing. "We will rather walk in the dark with God, than go alone in the light. We would rather walk with Him by faith, than walk alone by sight."

Among the Alps when day is done and darkness covers all the land, Mont Rosa and Mont Blanc rise up far above the darkness, catching from the retreating sun its light, now flushed with rose-color, exquisite beyond all words or pencil or paint, glowing like two pillars that form the Gate to Heaven.

So on these pages you will find the tall saints who rise above the mists of darkness around us and we behold their steady radiance drawn from beyond the western hills— the Son of righteousness. God grant that these may help restrain the dismal darkness that surrounds us and bring us rest and consolation.

May His Counsels Sweet uphold you,
    And His Loving Arms enfold you,
As you journey on your way.

May His Sheltering Wings protect you,
    And His Light Divine direct you,
Turning darkness into day.

May His Potent Peace surround you,
    And His Presence linger with you,
As your living golden ray.

N. A. Woychuk

Do Not Count
the Years

Finally, brethren,
whatever things are true,
whatever things are noble,
whatever things are just,
whatever things are pure,
whatever things are lovely,
whatever things are of good report,
if there is any virtue and
if there is anything praiseworthy—
meditate on these things.

Philippians 4:8

*Y*outh is not entirely a time of life; it is a state of mind. It is not wholly a matter of ripe cheeks, red lips, or supple knees. It is a temper of the will, a quality of the imagination, a vigor of the emotions. . .nobody grows old by merely living a number of years. People grow old only by deserting their ideals.

You are as young as your faith, as old as your doubt; as young as your self-confidence, as old as your fear; as young as your hope, as old as your despair.

In the central place of every heart there is a recording chamber. So long as it receives a message of beauty, hope, cheer, and courage— so long are you young. When the wires are all down and your heart is covered with the snow of pessimism and the ice of cynicism, then, and only then, are you grown old.

GENERAL DOUGLAS MACARTHUR,
on his seventy-fifth birthday

GROW OLD
ALONG WITH ME

*But the path of the just is like
the shining sun, that shines ever brighter
unto the perfect day.*
PROVERBS 4:18

Grow old along with me!
The best is yet to be,
The last of life, for which the first was made.
Our times are in His hand
Who saith, "A whole I planned,
Youth shows but half; trust God: see all,
        nor be afraid!

Then, welcome each rebuff
That turns earth's smoothness rough,

Each sting that bids nor sit nor stand but go!
Be our joys three-parts pain!

What I aspired to be,
And was not, comforts me:

ROBERT BROWNING
(1812–1889)

ME, MYSELF, AND MY TOMORROWS

*Now may the God of hope fill you with
all joy and peace in believing.*
ROMANS 15:13

Czech philosopher and martyr Viteslav Gardavsky wrote, "The terrible threat against life is not death, nor pain, nor any variation on the disasters that we obsessively try to protect ourselves against with our social systems and personal stratagems. The terrible threat is 'that we might die earlier than we really do die,' before death has become a natural necessity. The real horror lies in just such a premature death, a death after which we go on living for many years."[2]

Somewhere between age forty and fifty-five people begin to realize that the years they have already lived are undoubtedly more than the years that lie ahead. They tend to reflect on what life for them has been all about. They take a life inventory on what has had a positive or negative effect on their own growth and the growth of others. They decide, sometimes quite subconsciously, what to correct, adjust, or eliminate. Fred Smith wrote, "In middle life you don't want to make a junk yard out of your old age."[3]

Americans, however, need a word of caution. Our youth-oriented nation likes what is young; we avoid whatever smacks of decline or decrepitude. Gerontophobia—cringing at the thought of physical and mental impotence—has permeated our culture. Solomon's warning echoes menacingly, "Remember also your Creator in the days of your youth" (Ecclesiastes 12:1 NASB). Focusing on our Creator adds a new dimension of life. We do not grow old with age; we age because we are not growing.

To begin, we must blast before we build, erase before we establish the essentials of personal later-life management. A fistful of myths about old age need to be stifled. A myth is an oft-repeated belief that has no factual basis, but is generally accepted as true. Here are five such myths.

- First, that the closing years of life will inevitably be less enjoyable and stimulating than earlier years.

- Second, that old age is a disease, synonymous with disability and ill health.

- Third, that the ability to change or to absorb new ideas or learn new skills necessarily diminishes with age.

- Fourth, that new relationships are difficult or even impossible to form and maintain in old age.

- Fifth, that if you live long enough, you will be senile.

  Each one of these is wrong—a myth, a

false idea! It is possible to grow older and never get old. Contrary to accepted folklore, God does reserve the best for the last. However, an enjoyable and fruitful old age is not automatic. Each phase of life prepares for the next as we intentionally leave the past behind and step courageously ahead.

We are always fueling what is ahead; today gains glory only as it was seeded yesterday. Jesus said, "Unless a grain of wheat falls into the earth and dies, it remains by itself alone; but if it dies, it bears much fruit" (John 12:24 NASB). New life springs forth. We must get ready to get old.

How we think, what we are, and what we do now will formulate tomorrow. Reuel Howe reminds us, "Our insurance against tomorrow is what we do today."

The tenses of life—past, present, and future—are inseparable, says Ted Engstrom: "We cannot live entirely in the present without destroying the future, nor entirely in the future without destroying the present. . . . It is only to the degree that you are able to enjoy the present moment of life that you will be able to enjoy the future."

What you will be you are now becoming. The future does not contain within itself any miraculous elixir that will enable you to enjoy it. Enjoyment is an art that has to be learned in the present.

BIBLIOTHECA SACRA[4]

THE VINTAGE OF THE WESTERN SLOPES

*You crown the year with Your goodness,
and Your paths drip with abundance.*
PSALM 65:11

*T*is true that the eyes are somewhat dim
And the step not quite so fast,
But the blessing cup is filled to the brim
And life's best wine is the last.

For the vintage of the western slopes
Has a fragrance all its own
From the gathered memories and hopes
That the summer suns have grown.

And so I sing of the beautiful years,
Each one with God's goodness crowned
And better far than my foolish fears
Were the months and the seasons found.

ANONYMOUS

I'VE ONLY BEGUN TO LIVE

*For a thousand years in Your sight
are like yesterday.*
(PSALM 90:4)

Although we're living in a day when medical science is extending the span of human life, the numbers mentioned in Psalm 90:10 still express the general rule: "The days of our lives are seventy years; and if by reason of strength they are eighty years, yet their boast is only labor and sorrow." There is, however, no need for believers who are approaching those years to become depressed. Rather than dreading the sunset of this life, they should be anticipating the sunrise of the next.

D. L. Moody, in the book *Daily Gems*, related the following experience: "I was down in Texas some time ago, and happened to pick up a newspaper, and there they called me 'Old Moody.' Honestly, I never got such a shock from any paper in my life! I had never been called old before. I went to my hotel and looked in the mirror. I cannot conceive of getting old. I have a life that is never going to end. Death may change my position but not my condition, not my standing with Jesus Christ. . . . If you meet me ten million years hence, then I will be young. . . . Don't call me old. I am only sixty-two. I have only begun to live!"

As a believer with an eternity before you, no matter what your age—whether you're a child, a young adult, middle-aged, or even in your sixties, seventies, or eighties—the best still lies ahead. That should put joy in your heart, a smile on your face, and a song on your lips. Every Christian is blessed with a long life—it's everlasting!

Immortality is the glorious capstone of Christianity.

R. W. DeHaan[5]

Not Knowing

For we walk by faith, not by sight.
2 Corinthians 5:7

I know not what shall befall me,
  God hangs a mist o'er my eyes;
And so each step in my onward path He
  makes new scenes to rise,
And every joy He sends me, comes as a
  strange and sweet surprise.

I see not a step before me, as I tread on
  another year,
But the past is still in God's keeping, the
  future His mercy shall clear:
And what looks dark in the distance, may
  brighten as I draw near—

It may be He has waited for the coming of
    my feet,
Some gift of such rare blessedness, some joy
    so strangely sweet,
That my lips shall only tremble with the
    thanks they cannot speak.

Oh! restful, blissful ignorance! 'Tis blessed
    not to know,
It keeps me so still in those arms which will
    not let me go,
And hushes my soul to rest in the bosom
    that loves me so!

So I go on not knowing; I would not if I
    might.
I would rather walk in the dark with God,
    than go alone in the light.
I would rather walk with Him by faith,
    than walk alone by sight.

CONGREGATIONALIST

I WILL HOPE CONTINUALLY

*B*ut I will hope continually, and will praise You yet more and more. My mouth shall tell of Your righteousness and Your salvation all the day, for I do not know their limits. I will go in the strength of the Lord GOD; I will make mention of Your righteousness, of Yours only.

O God, You have taught me from my youth; and to this day I declare Your wondrous works. Now also when I am old and grayheaded, O God, do not forsake me, until I declare Your strength to this generation, Your power to everyone who is to come.

PSALM 71:14–18

How Firm a Foundation

For no other foundation can anyone lay
than that which is laid,
which is Jesus Christ.
1 Corinthians 3:11

*A*ffirming the Bible as man's only sure hope and anchor, this hymn's final four stanzas are imbedded with potent Scripture. The lyrics say it all:

Fear not, I am with Thee; O be not
dismayed,
For I am thy God, and will still give
thee aid; I'll
strengthen thee, help thee, and cause
thee to stand,

*upheld by My righteous, omnipotent
    hand.*

These lines are based on
Isaiah 41:10.

*When through the deep waters I call
    thee to go,
The rivers of woe shall not thee over-
    flow; for I will
be with thee thy troubles to bless and
    sanctify to thee thy deepest distress.*

These lines are based on
Isaiah 43:2.

*When through fiery trials thy pathway
    shall lie,
My grace, all sufficient, shall be thy
    supply: The flame
shall not hurt thee. I only design, thy
    dross to consume
and thy gold to refine.*

These lines are based on
2 Corinthians 12:9.

The soul that on Jesus hath leaned for repose I will
not, I will not desert to its foes; that soul, though all
hell should endeavor to shake, I'll never, no, never,
no, never forsake!

These lines are based on
HEBREWS 13:5.

GLADYS TEAGUE

Sweet to Reflect

What shall I render to the LORD
for all His benefits toward me?
PSALM 116:12

Sweet to look back, and see my name
In Life's fair book set down;
Sweet to look forward, and behold
Eternal joys my own.

Sweet to reflect, how grace divine
My sins on Jesus laid;
Sweet to remember that His blood
My debt of sufferings paid.

Sweet on His righteousness to stand,
Which saves from second death;

Sweet to experience, day by day,
His spirit's quickening breath.

Sweet on His faithfulness to rest,
Whose love can never end;
Sweet on His covenant of grace
For all things to depend.

These eyes shall see Him in that day,
The God that died for me!
And all my rising bones shall say,
Lord, who is like to Thee?

If such the views which grace unfolds,
Weak as it is below,
What raptures must the Church above
In Jesus' presence know!

O, may the unction of these truths
Forever with me stay,
Till, from her sinful cage dismissed,
My spirit flies away!

A. M. Toplady
(1740–1778)

AND STILL GROWING

Consider the lilies of the field,
how they grow.
MATTHEW 6:28

Consider the lilies of the field,
How trustfully they grow;
Their glowing chalices have not been
    wrought
By anxious toil, nor have they taken
    thought
How they shall thrive; but, tall and fair,
They drink the sunlight and the air,
Each from God's hand,
As He has planned;
And so the lilies grow.

Consider the lilies of the field,

How peacefully they grow;
Their Father's love and care they
    question not,
Nor murmur at their own apportioned lot.
The sun and storm to them fulfil
God's thought for them. All is His will.
God's way is best;
They leave the rest;
And so the lilies grow.

Consider the lilies of the field,
How royally they grow.
Not even Solomon, in king's array,
Was clad like one of these, which, for a day,
Lives to praise God, then, scorched and
    dried,
Its glory gone, is cast aside.
Clothed by God's hand,
Their beauty planned—
'Tis thus the lilies grow.

Consider the lilies of the field,
How exemplary they grow.
If God so cares for them and makes
    them fair

For their brief day, shall He not much
    more care,
O ye of little faith, for you?
His tender mercies still are new;
Then trust His love
And look above,
E'en as the lilies grow.

MINNIE E. PAULL

Age Is Opportunity

They shall still bear fruit in old age;
they shall be fresh and flourishing.
Psalm 92:14

Something remains for us to do or dare;
even the oldest tree some fruit may bear. . .
For age is opportunity no less than youth
    itself,
though in another dress,
and as the evening twilight fades away,
the sky is filled with stars, invisible by day!

Henry Wadsworth Longfellow
(1807–1882)

Inward Peace
and Inward Might

You will keep him in perfect peace,
whose mind is stayed on You,
because he trusts in You.
Isaiah 26:3

Courage, brother, do not stumble,
Though thy path be dark as night;
There's a star to guide the humble;—
"Trust in God, and do the right."

Let the road be rough and dreary,
And its end far out of sight,
Foot it bravely! strong, or weary,
"Trust in God, and do the right."

Perish policy and cunning!
Perish all the fears the light!
Whether losing, whether winning,
"Trust in God, and do the right!"

Trust no party, sect, or faction;
Trust no leaders in the fight;
But in every word and action,
"Trust in God, and do the right."

Trust no lovely forms of passion:
Friends may look like angels bright;
Trust no custom, school, or fashion,
"Trust in God, and do the right."

Simple rule, and safest guiding,
Inward peace, and inward might,
Star upon our path abiding,
"Trust in God, and do the right."

Some will hate thee, some will love thee
Some will flatter, some will slight:
Cease from man, and look above thee,
"Trust in God, and do the right."

NORMAN MCLEOD

COMMUNION WITH GOD

Walk in the light as He is in the light.
1 JOHN 1:7

There is no loneliness like that which accompanies human sorrow. The gentle, persuasive sympathy of friends cannot dissipate it; communion with nature cannot shake off its pall; recourse to intellectual activity cannot diminish its heaviness; and allurements of the world or of the secular life tend rather to emphasize it.

The supreme cure for heart loneliness is communion with God; and it seems sometimes as if only by means of the loneliness which sorrow brings do we come to appreciate the value, satisfaction, and real meaning of intercourse with the divine Father. At such times we may have a clearer knowledge of His purpose, a more definite comprehension of the divine economy, a higher conception of our own relation to that purpose and economy, and out of it all may come a more settled determination to devote ourselves to the cause of God and the service of mankind. It requires loneliness sometimes to convince us that we are not alone, and the darkness to show us the light.

To one who is in complete harmony with God, and who enjoys the blessings of communion with Him, the things that seem mysterious in His dealings with His children have all a beneficent meaning; the things that seem contradictory and inconsistent with a kind and considerate nature are all acknowledged to be right and reasonable, even though their immediate necessity may not be apparent; and the things that have brought sorrow, or loneliness, or distress, or disappointment, or pain are all revealed as the objects of a sublime and holy purpose, and are accepted as having their place among the "all things" which work together for good to them that love God.

CHRISTIAN AGE

THE HAPPY SOUL

Rejoice in the Lord always.
Again I will say, rejoice!
PHILIPPIANS 4:4

O happy soul, that lives on high,
While men lie groveling here!
His hopes are fixed above the sky,
And faith forbids his fear.

His conscience knows no secret stings;
While peace and joy combine
To form a life, whose holy springs
Are hidden and divine.

His pleasures rise from things unseen,
Beyond this world and time,

Where neither eyes nor ears have been,
Nor thoughts of sinners climb.

He looks to heaven's eternal hill,
To meet that glorious day;
And patient waits His Savior's will,
To fetch his soul away.

Isaac Watts
(1674–1748)

The Ages
Come and Go

For I am the LORD,
I do not change.
MALACHI 3:6

The ages come and go,
The centuries pass as years,
And Him evermore I behold,
Walking in Galilee,
Thro' the cornfield's waving gold,
In hamlet, in wood and in wold,
By the shores of the beautiful sea.
He touches the sightless eyes;
Before Him the demons flee;
To the dead He says: Arise!
To the living: Follow Me!

And that Voice still soundeth on
From the centuries that are gone
To the centuries that shall be!

UNKNOWN

WITH THEE IS REST

As one whom his mother comforts,
so I will comfort you.
ISAIAH 66:13

O God, a world of empty show,
Dark wilds of restless, fruitless quest,
Lie round me wheresoe'er I go:
Within, with Thee, is rest.

And sated with the weary sum
Of all men think, and hear, and see,
O more than mother's heart, I come
A tired child to Thee.

Sweet childhood of eternal life!
Whilst troubled days and years go by,

In stillness hushed from stir and strife
Within Thine Arms I lie.

Thine Arms, to whom I turn and cling
With thirsting soul that longs for Thee—
As rain that makes the pastures sing
Be Thou my God, to me.

GERHARD TERSTEEGEN
(1697–1769)

I Know!

For I know whom I have believed.
2 Timothy 1:12

In the early days of World War II, I was a theological student in Bristol. At that time, Sir Walford Davies was conducting a daily broadcast service from the Cathedral. It was a never-to-be-forgotten experience watching Sir Walford blend the voices of a team of singers for half an hour in preparation for the devotional service which would bring spiritual uplift to millions.

On Ordination Day I spied the great musician in the congregation. I would soon be leaving England for Australia and would possibly never again see him. Approaching him, I smiled my introduction as one of the

newly ordained men and one who had enjoyed so much his informal talks from time
to time in recent weeks. I asked him for his
autograph and as the Greek New Testament,
the Ordination Gift of the Bishop of Bristol
was the only book I had, I asked him to
inscribe his signature beneath that of the
Bishop.

For a moment he stood thinking, then he
hummed the two notes, soh-doh.

"Yes," he replied, "I will give you the two
greatest notes of music. They are the notes
with which Handel penned his recitative in
the Messiah, *'I know* that my Redeemer
liveth.' Here they are," and softly but firmly
he sang the words, *"I know."* Rapidly he
drew the five lines of the staff notation in
the flyleaf of my New Testament, and wrote
in the two notes.

After signing it, he returned the book to
me, and placing his hands on my shoulder,
Sir Walford Davies, Musician to the King,
master of the art of making music, minister
to the needs of the worshipper, nearing as he
was the end of his life's work, said to me, a

young man on the threshold of his ministry, "We are both occupied in the same task from different angles. All good wishes for your future, my boy, and may these two notes form the theme of your message—*'I know.'* "

The Australian Church Record

A Prayer

*A word fitly spoken is like apples of gold
in settings of silver.*
PROVERBS 25:11

Lord, Thou knowest better than I
know myself that I am growing
older, and will someday be old.

Keep me from getting talkative
and particularly from the fatal
habit of thinking that I must say
something on every subject and on
every occasion.

Release me from craving to try to
straighten out everybody's affairs.

Keep my mind free from the recital of endless details—give me wings to get to the point.

I ask for grace enough to listen to the tales of others' pains. Help me to endure them with patience.

But seal my lips on my own aches and pains. They are increasing and my love of rehearsing them is becoming sweeter as the years go by.

Teach me the glorious lesson that occasionally it is possible that I may be mistaken.

Keep me reasonably sweet, I do not want to be a saint—some of them are so hard to live with—but a sour person is one of the crowning works of the devil.

Make me thoughtful—but not moody: helpful but not bossy. With

my vast store of wisdom, it seems
such a pity not to use it all, but thou
knowest Lord, that I want a few
friends at the end. Amen.

Anonymous

THE LORD WILL PROVIDE

And my God shall supply all your need.
PHILIPPIANS 4:19

Though troubles assail us, and dangers
    afright,
Though friends should all fail us, and foes
    all unite,
Yet one thing secures us, whatever betide,
The promise assures us, "the Lord will
    provide."
The birds, without garner of storehouse,
    are fed;
From them let us learn to trust God for our
    bread:
His saints what is fitting shall ne'er be denied
So long as 'tis written, "the Lord will
    provide."

When Satan assails us to stop up our path,
And courage all fails us, we triumph by
　　faith.
He cannot take from us, though oft he has
　　tried,
This heart cheering promise, "the Lord will
　　provide."
No strength of our own, and no goodness
　　we claim;
Yet, since we have known of the Savior's
　　great Name,
In this our strong tower for safety we hide:
The Lord is our power, "the Lord will
　　provide."

JOHN NEWTON
(1725–1807)

CAN YOU REMEMBER

*Come to Me, all you who labor and
are heavy laden, and I will give you rest.*
MATTHEW 11:28

Prudence: "Can you remember by what
means you find your annoyances at
times as if they were vanquished?"

Christian: "Yes; when I think what I saw at
the cross, that will do it; and when I
look upon my broidered coat, that will
do it; and when I look into the roll that
I carry in my bosom, that will do it; and
when my thoughts wax warm about
whither I am going, that will do it."

Prudence: "And what is it that makes you so desirous to go to Mount Zion?"

Christian: "Why, there I hope to see Him alive that did hang dead on the cross; and there I hope to be rid of all those things that to this day are in me an annoyance to me: there they say there is no death, and there I shall dwell with such company as I like best. For, to tell you truth, I love Him because I was by Him eased of my burden; and I am weary of my inward sickness. I would fain be where I shall die no more and with the company that shall continually cry, Holy, holy, holy."

JOHN BUNYAN
(1628–1688)
from *The Pilgrim's Progress*

UNPREMEDITATED ART

Look at the birds of the air.
MATTHEW 6:26

The English skylark described in this poem, "To a Skylark," awakens with the rising sun and sings as it mounts higher and higher upon its wings, as if it were bidding earth adieu. "It had gone to mingle with the choirs of heaven," says Jeremy Taylor; even when this "spirit-bird" is entirely lost to vision its glad notes continue to flood back to earth like the music of an angel.

Hail to thee, blithe spirit!
Bird thou never wert,
That from heaven, or near it,
Pourest thy full heart

In profuse strains of unpremeditated
    art.

Higher still and higher,
From the earth thou springest
Like a cloud of fire;
The blue deep thou wingest,
And singing still dost soar, and soaring
    ever singest.

Like a poet hidden
In the light of thought,
Singing hymns unbidden,
Till the world is wrought
To sympathy with hopes and fears it
    heeded not:

Like a high-born maiden
In a palace tower,
Soothing her love-laden
Soul in secret hour
With music sweet as love, which over-
    flows her bower:

Like a glow-worm golden
In a dell of dew,

Scattering unbeholden
Its aerial hue
Among the flowers and grass, which
 screen it from the view:

Like a rose embowered
In its own green leaves,
By warm winds deflowered,
Till the scent it gives
Makes faint with too much sweet those
 heavy-winged thieves:

What objects are the fountains
Of thy happy strain?
What fields, or waves, or mountains?
What shapes of sky or plain?
What love of thine own kind? What
 ignorance of pain?

Waking as asleep,
Thou of death must deem
Things more true and deep
Than we mortals dream,
Or how could thy notes flow in such a
 crystal stream?

We look before and after,
And pine for what is not:
Our sincerest laughter
With some pain is fraught;
Our sweetest songs are those that tell of
    saddest thought.

Teach me half the gladness
That thy brain must know,
Such harmonious madness
From my lips would flow,
The world should listen then, as I am
    listening now.

PERCY BYSSHE SHELLEY
(1792–1822)

TODAY

Stand still, and see the salvation of the LORD,
which He will accomplish for you today.
EXODUS 14:13

*T*oday, I will do today's work, with today's light, today's comfort, today's help,
whether in spirit direct from God, or through
means of His choosing and using. My rule is
for today. My promise from Him is for today. My trust is for now. I will not look
beyond today. I will do right today; pray,
trust, rejoice, praise all today, and again tomorrow, when it becomes today, till that day
dawns which will have no night.

CHRISTIAN TREASURY

LET GOD PLAN FOR YOU

My times are in Your hand.
PSALM 31:15

These are Christ's words, for the psalm is one of His utterances when bearing our sins. He is speaking as the "sent" one—the dependent, trusting Son of man.

We too can take up these words. We look up and remember Jehovah. What He is, even apart from what He is to us, is our joy. He is Jehovah; He is the disposer of times and events, the sovereign arranger of everything relating to us. We are creatures, sinners, worms; yet He is so condescendingly mindful of us that He orders our whole life and lot. He in whose hand our times are is the God of love.

- What solemnity, then, does this cast over life! A life thus wholly ordered in all its times by the infinite Jehovah must be a solemn thing.

- What stability does it impart! Even in such an unstable world everything is under the regulation of an unchanging purpose.

- What certainty does it give to all that passes! There can be no random, nay, no trivial events; nothing disjointed or loose.

- What peace does it fill us with in this tempestuous age! Empires may rock to and fro, statesmen stagger, confusion reign; we are at peace. All is well.

- What consolation in sorrow! Our times are in hands divinely wise and powerful. All must work for good. There can be no real evil.

- What hope for the future! We know
  that there is light beyond this
  gloom. The storm is for an hour; the
  calm that follows is eternal.

HORATIUS BONAR
(1808–1889)

THE PATH I HAVE PREPARED FOR YOU

You will show me the path of life.
PSALM 16:11

The pathway you see is the path I have chosen and prepared for you. Follow it with confidence, trust, and courage. It will perfectly lead you into the plans I have for your life. If you ever wonder where the pathway is taking you, simply look down and you will notice My footsteps ahead of you and behind you.

As you walk you will notice other pathways close to yours. Some will draw your interest and curiosity. You may be attracted because of flowers that border them, trees that shade them, or the direction in which they are heading. What you don't see is the depth of the valleys, and the steepness of the mountains through which they wind. Those whom I have called to travel these other pathways will have My grace for their journey. I do not want you to waste your time imagining what it might be like traveling down someone else's path. If you choose another's path, you will not have My grace upon you, and the valleys and hills will burden you and create a weariness within you.

The time and energy I give you will always be enough for each day's travel, and you will find many resting places along the way. Give yourself completely to the path I have prepared for you. As you do, continue to look upon My face, for My smile will be upon you. Never forget that everything is significant and working together for the good. I know where the path will take you, for I have already traveled it. Believe Me when I say that you can never imagine the incredible things that await you.

ROY LESSIN[6]

If We Could See
Beyond Today

*And God will wipe away every tear
from their eyes.*
Revelation 21:4

If we could see beyond today as God
 can see,
If all the clouds should roll away, the
 shadows flee;
O'er present griefs we would not fret, each
 sorrow we would soon forget,
For many joys are waiting yet for you and me.

If we could know beyond today as God
 doth know,
Why dearest treasures pass away, and tears
 must flow;

And why the darkness leads to light, why
    dreary days will soon grow bright,
Some day life's wrongs will be made right,
    faith tells us so.

If we could see, if we could know, we often
    say,
But God in love a veil doth throw across
    our way;
We cannot see what lies before, and so we
    cling to Him the more,
He leads us till this life is o'er, trust and
    obey.

Author Unknown

SOME TIME
WE'LL UNDERSTAND

As for me,
I will see Your face in righteousness;
I shall be satisfied when I awake in
Your likeness.
PSALM 17:15

Not now, but in the coming years,
It may be in the better land,
We'll read the meaning of our tears,
And there, some time, we'll understand.

Then trust in God thro' all the days;
Fear not, for He doth hold thy hand;
Though dark thy way, still sing and praise,
Some time, some time, we'll understand.

We'll catch the broken thread again,
And finish what we here began;
Heav'n will the mysteries explain,
And then, ah, then, we'll understand.

We'll know why clouds instead of sun
Were over many a cherished plan;
Why song has ceased when scarce begun;
'Tis there, some time, we'll understand.

God knows the way, He holds the key,
He guides us with unerring hand;
Some time with tearless eyes we'll see;
Yes, there, up there, we'll understand.

MAXWELL N. CORNELIUS

In the very nature of the case, it is of necessity that finite man should fail at some point to comprehend the infinite God. Faith follows on, walking with God, even when reason fails to comprehend. Faith trusts God in the dark. That is, after reason has entered into darkness and obscurity, faith goes on, walking—not in darkness, but in the light of

God, because she trusts in God.

Otherwise, faith need not be at all, for to walk by faith is essentially opposed to walking by sight. When sight comes in, there is no further need for faith.

Let us thank God for the privilege of trusting Him, and of walking quietly with Him, leaving our hand in His, for, though we may not know, it is always true that He knoweth the way that we take.

William Pettinghill

LET THE BEAUTY OF THE LORD OUR GOD BE UPON US

*O*h, satisfy us early with Your mercy, that
we may rejoice and be glad all our days!
Make us glad according to the days in
which You have afflicted us, the years
in which we have seen evil. Let Your work
appear to Your servants, and Your glory
to their children. And let the beauty of
the LORD our God be upon us, and
establish the work of our hands for us;
yes, establish the work of our hands.

PSALM 90:14–17

Because he has set his love upon Me, therefore I will deliver him; I will set him on
high, because he has known My name.
He shall call upon Me, and I will
answer him; I will be with him in trouble; I will deliver him and honor him.

Psalm 91:14, 15

The righteous shall flourish like a palm tree,
he shall grow like a cedar in Lebanon.
Those who are planted in the house of
the LORD shall flourish in the courts of
our God. They shall still bear fruit in
old age; they shall be fresh and flourishing, to declare that the LORD is upright;
He is my rock, and there is no unright-
eousness in Him.

Psalm 92:12–15

Rest

And He said to them,
"Come aside by yourselves to a deserted place
and rest a while."

MARK 6:31

There is no music in a "rest," but there is the making of music in it.

In our whole life melody, the music is broken off here and there by "rests" and we foolishly think we have come to the end of the tune. God sends a time (or "there seems to be a time") of forced leisure, sickness, disappointed plans, frustrated efforts that makes a sudden pause in the choral hymn of our lives, and we lament that our voice must be silent and our part missing in the music which ever goes up to the ear of the Creator.

How does the musician read the rest?

See him beat the time with unvarying count, and catch up the next note true and steady, as if no breaking place had come in between.

Not without design does God write the music of our lives. But be it ours to learn the time and not be dismayed at the "rests." They are not to be slurred over, not to be omitted, nor to destroy the melody, nor to change the keynote.

If we look up, God Himself will beat the time for us. With the eye on Him, we shall strike the next note, full and clear.

AUTHOR UNKNOWN

Trusting in My Father's Wise Bestowment

*Whoever trusts in the LORD
shall be safe.*
PROVERBS 29:25

Day by day, and with each passing moment,
Strength I find to meet my trials here;
Trusting in my Father's wise bestowment,
I've no cause for worry or for fear.
He, whose heart is kind beyond all measure,
Gives unto each day what He deems best,
Lovingly its part of pain and pleasure,
Mingling toil with peace and rest.

Every day the Lord Himself is near me,
With a special mercy for each hour;

All my cares He fain would bear and
    cheer me,
He whose name is Counsellor and Pow'r.
The protection of His child and treasure
Is a charge that on Himself He laid;
"As thy days, thy strength shall be in
    measure,"
This the pledge to me He made.

Help me then, in every tribulation,
So to trust Thy promises, O Lord,
That I lose not faith's sweet consolation,
Offered me within Thy holy Word.
Help me, Lord, when toil and trouble
    meeting,
E'er to take, as from a father's hand,
One by one, the days, the moments
    fleeting,
Till I reach the promised land.

LINA SANDELL
(1832–1903)

If My Days
Were Untroubled

It is good for me that I have been afflicted,
that I may learn Your statutes.
PSALM 119:71

If my days were untroubled, and my
   heart always light,
Would I seek that fair land where there is
   no night?

If I never grew weary with the weight of my
   load,
Would I search for God's peace at the end
   of the road?

If I never knew sickness and never felt pain,
Would I search for a land to help and sustain?

If I walked not with sorrow and lived with-
    out loss,
Would my soul seek sweet solace at the foot
    of the cross?

If all I desired was mine day by day,
Would I kneel before God and earnestly
    pray?

If God sent no Winter to freeze me with
    fear,
Would I yearn for the warmth of Spring
    every year?

I ask myself this, and the answer is plain—
If my life were all pleasure and I never
    knew pain—

I'd seek God less often and need Him much
    less,
For God is sought more often in times of
    distress.

And no one knows God or sees Him as
    plain

As those who have met Him on the
"Pathway of Pain."

AUTHOR UNKNOWN

THINK THROUGH ME
THOUGHTS OF GOD

For I know the thoughts that I think toward
you, says the LORD, thoughts of peace and not
of evil, to give you a future and a hope.
JEREMIAH 29:11

Think through me thoughts of God,
My Father quiet me;
Till in Thy holy presence hushed,
I think Thy thoughts with Thee.

Sing through me songs of God,
My Father quiet me;
Till in Thy holy presence hushed,
I sing Thy songs with Thee.

AMY CARMICHAEL[7]

He Maketh No Mistake

As for God, His way is perfect.
PSALM 18:30

My Father's way may twist and turn,
My heart may throb and ache,
But in my soul I'm glad to know,
He maketh no mistake.

My cherished plans may go astray,
My hopes may fade away,
But still I'll trust my Lord to lead,
For He doth know the way.

Tho' night be dark and it may seem
That day will never break,
I'll pin my faith, my all, in Him;
He maketh no mistake.

There's so much now I cannot see,
My eyesight far too dim,
But come what may, I'll simply trust
And leave it all to Him.

For bye and bye the mist will lift,
And plain it all He'll make.
Through all the way, tho' dark to me,
He made not one mistake.

Author Unknown

A HEART AT LEISURE FROM ITSELF

You will keep him in perfect peace,
whose mind is stayed on You.
ISAIAH 26:3

Father, I know that all my life
Is portioned out for me,
And the changes that are sure to come,
I do not fear to see;
But I ask Thee for a present mind,
Intent on pleasing Thee.

I ask Thee for a thoughtful love,
Through constant watching wise,
To meet the glad with joyful smiles,
And wipe the weeping eyes;

And a heart at leisure from itself,
To soothe and sympathize.

I would not have the restless will
That hurries to and fro,
Seeking for some great thing to do,
Or secret thing to know;
I would be treated as a child,
And guided where I go.

So I ask Thee for the daily strength,
To none that ask denied,
And a mind to blend with outward life,
While keeping at Thy side;
Content to fill a little space,
If Thou be glorified.

ANNA LETITIA WARING
(1823–1910)

RE-IGNITED

But His word was in my heart
like a burning fire.
JEREMIAH 20:9

When John Knox took Scotland for God, he was in his early fifties, but apparently as he was living in his forties, life had flattened out for him, and in one of his journals, John Knox wrote something like this. He said,

> *I will keep the ground that God has given me, and perhaps in His grace He will ignite me again, but ignite me or not, by His grace, I will hold the ground.*

And that, I take it, is the commitment of

the middle years. When life does flatten out, when we find the going difficult, when we find the success that we had sought for wasn't really the success we wanted—during those years, when things are much less emotional and we are depressed and feeling sorry for ourselves and recognize that we are mortal and know that we are going to die, that is the committal of faith. Not as drastic as the battles of youth, but every bit as necessary.

I will keep the ground that God has given me, and perhaps in His grace He will ignite me again, but ignite me or not, by His grace I will hold the ground.

HADDON ROBINSON[8]

Not Time Enough

My days are swifter than a weaver's shuttle.
JOB 7:6

$\mathcal{L}$ife is a short and fevered rehearsal for a concert we cannot stay to give. Just when we appear to have attained some proficiency we are forced to lay our instruments down. There is simply not time enough to think, to become, to perform what we are capable of.

How completely satisfying to turn from our limitations to a God Who has none. Eternal years lie in His heart. For Him, time does not pass, it remains; and those who are in Christ share with Him all the riches of limitless time, and endless years.

A. W. TOZER

THE WEST WINDS BLOW

But those who wait on the LORD
shall renew their strength.
ISAIAH 40:31

I mourn no more my vanished years;
Beneath a tender rain,
An April rain of smiles and tears,
My heart is young again.

The west winds blow, and singing low,
I hear the glad streams run;
The windows of my soul I throw
Wide open to the sun.

No longer forward, nor behind,
I look in hope and fear;

But grateful, take the good I find,
The best of now, and here.

I plow no more a desert land
For harvest, weed and tare;
The manna dropping from God's hand,
Rebukes my painful care.

Enough that blessings undeserved,
Have marked my erring track;
That wheresoe'er my feet have swerved,
His chastening turned me back.

That more and more a providence
Of love is understood,
Making the springs of time and sense,
Sweet with eternal good.

That death seems but a covered way,
Which opens into light;
Wherein no blinded child can stray
Beyond the Father's sight.

That care and trial seem at last,
Through memory's sunset air,

Like mountain ranges overpast
In purple distance fair.

That all the jarring notes of life
Seem blending in a psalm,
And all the angels of its strife,
Slow rounding into calm.

And so the shadows fall apart,
And so the west winds play;
And all the windows of my heart
I open to this day.

John G. Whittier
(1807–1892)

DELIGHTING IN THE WORD
OF THE LORD

He shall be like a tree
planted by the rivers of water,
that brings forth its fruit in its season.

PSALM 1:3

Peter Waldo (1140–1217) is remembered as the founder of the Waldenses, the group that endured such bloody persecutions for centuries in the Italian and French Alps. Waldo was a great Christian leader, and among other things he gave the people of southern Europe the Scriptures in their own tongue, the Romaunt version of the Bible. He left a great legacy, not only to the Waldenses but to all believers.

He must have seemed to his followers and friends like a spring from which constantly flowed a refreshing stream of holy Scripture. For every occasion and in every situation he always had the right Bible verse. In the heat of conflict, he would exhort the people, "Finally, my brethren, be strong in the Lord and in the power of His might" (Ephesians 6:10), and he would comfort them with 2 Corinthians 4:17, "For our light affliction, which is but for a moment, is working for us a far more exceeding and eternal weight of glory."

Waldo's work laid the foundation for the great Reformation. As always, people were in desperate need of instruction and inspiration. Waldo drew heavily upon Psalm 19 and Psalm 119: "The statutes of the LORD are right, rejoicing the heart; the commandment of the LORD is pure, enlightening the eyes; the fear of the LORD is clean, enduring forever; the judgments of the LORD are true and righteous altogether. More to be desired are they than gold, yea, than much fine gold; sweeter also than honey and the honeycomb"; "You, through Your commandments, make me wiser than my enemies; for they are ever with me. I have more understanding than all my teachers, for Your testimonies are my meditation."

Trouble and depression often plagued the believers who were so continually exposed to opposition and persecution. Peter Waldo often comforted them by leading them in thoughtful meditation on Psalm 23:

> The LORD is my shepherd; I shall not want.
> He makes me to lie down in green pastures;
> He leads me beside the still waters.
> He restores my soul;
> He leads me in the paths of righteousness for His name's sake.
> Yea, though I walk through the valley of the shadow of death,
> I will fear no evil; for You are with me.

When surrounded by distress and fear, he could be heard pouring out his heart in Scripture: "I would have lost heart, unless I had believed that I would see the goodness of the LORD in the land of the living. Wait on the LORD; be of good courage, and He shall strengthen your heart; wait, I say, on the LORD" (Psalm 27:13, 14). Then he would lead the despairing believers in humble confession: "Purge me with hyssop, and I shall be clean; wash me, and I shall be whiter than snow. Make me hear joy and gladness, that the bones You have broken may rejoice. . . . Create in me a clean heart, O God, and renew a steadfast spirit within me. . . . Restore to me the joy of Your salvation, and uphold me by Your generous Spirit" (Psalm 51:7, 8, 10, 12).

Trusting the Lord was his most hard-fought battle. Many times he must have recalled Psalm 37:5: "Commit your way to the LORD, trust also in Him, and He shall bring it to pass." And then, speaking to himself, he would repeat softly, "Rest in the LORD, and wait patiently for Him" (Psalm 37:7). Often, one of the other believers, as if to remind them all, would speak out this verse from the Word: "Men always ought to pray and not lose heart" (Luke 18:1).

Through the most severe trials, this man of God, as if unconscious of the presence of others, would recall out loud Peter's triumphant words: "Blessed be the God and Father of our Lord Jesus Christ, who according to His abundant mercy has begotten us again to a living hope through the resurrection of Jesus Christ from the dead, to an inheritance incorruptible and undefiled and that does not fade away, reserved in heaven for you, who are kept by the power of God through faith for salvation ready to be revealed in the last time. In this you greatly rejoice, though now for a little while, if need be, you have been grieved by various trials, that the genuineness of your faith, being much more precious than gold that perishes, though it is tested by fire, may be found to praise, honor, and glory at the revelation of Jesus Christ, whom having not seen you love. Though now you do not see Him, yet believing, you rejoice with joy inexpressible and full of glory" (1 Peter 1:3–8).

Often when his group was surrounded by a formidable enemy and the situation seemed hopeless, Peter thanked God for victory: "Now thanks be to God who always leads us in triumph in Christ, and through us diffuses the fragrance of His knowledge in every place" (2 Corinthians 2:14). Somehow he believed that God had everything under control, and he would boldly recite Romans 8:28, claiming the reality that all things work together for good to those who are called according to the Lord's purposes.

When a person is so steeped in the Word of God, he has a profound effect on those around him. His companions could not help but also drink in God's Word. This type of profound communion with God characterized the Waldenses for generations—from the thirteenth through the seventeenth centuries.

They did not keep their faith to themselves, however. Instead, they shared it with the world around them. The young men who followed Peter would go out among the people and peddle various articles. After a little confidence was established, the "peddler" would say, "I have jewels more precious than these things; I would make you a present of them if you would promise not to betray me to the clergy." Or the "peddler" would say with a radiant expression, "I have a pearl so brilliant that by it men may come to know God. . . . I have another so splendid that it kindles the love of God in the heart of the person who possesses it."

What a majestic moment it must have been when these believers gathered on frequent occasions and with deep devotion quoted Scripture together, praising and worshiping the Lord:

Bless the LORD, O my soul;
And all that is within me, bless His
    holy name!
Bless the LORD, O my soul,
And forget not all His benefits:
Who forgives all your iniquities,
Who heals all your diseases,
Who redeems your life from
    destruction,
Who crowns you with lovingkindness
    and tender mercies,

Who satisfies your mouth with good
things,
So that your youth is renewed like the
eagle's.

PSALM 103:1–5

Among these worshipers there were no
age barriers. Young and old alike flourished
like the palm tree. The Word of the Lord
dwelt richly in the hearts of both the old and
the young, and they all produced fruit, "some
a hundredfold, some sixty, some thirty."

We too can share their secret. Everyone—
like Peter Waldo, whose delight was in the
law of the Lord, and in whose law he medi-
tated day and night—can "be like a tree
planted by the rivers of water, that brings
forth its fruit in its season, whose leaf also
shall not wither; and whatever he does shall
prosper" (Psalm 1:3).

N. A. WOYCHUK

DELIGHT IN GOD ONLY

Delight yourself also in the LORD.
PSALM 37:4

This poem was written by a man who lived in the time of Charles I, whose cause he opposed. The opposing forces harassed this author, took away his books, and destroyed his manuscripts. This broke his health and troubled his spirit. Out of this experience, he wrote this poem.

I love (and have some cause to love) the
    earth;
She is my Maker's creature; therefore
    good:
She is my mother, for she gave me birth;

She is my tender nurse—she gives me
food;
But what's a creature, Lord, compared
with thee?
Or what's my mother, or my nurse to me?

I love the air: her dainty sweets refresh
My drooping soul, and to new sweets
invites me;
He shrill-mouthed quire sustains me
with their flesh,
And with their many-toned notes
delights me:
But what's the air or all the sweets that
she
Can bless my soul withal, compared to
thee?

I love the sea: she is my fellow-creature,
My careful purveyor; she provides me
store;
She walls me round; she makes my diet
greater;
She wafts my treasure from a foreign
shore:

But, Lord of oceans, when compared
with thee,
What is the ocean, or her wealth to me?

To heaven's high city I direct my
journey,
Whose spangled suburbs entertain
mine eye;
Mine eye, by contemplation's great
attorney,
Transcends the crystal pavement of
the sky:
But what is heaven, great God, compared to thee?
Without thy presence, heaven's no
heaven to me.

Without thy presence earth gives no
reflection;
Without thy presence sea affords no
treasure;
Without thy presence air's a rank
infection;
Without thy presence heaven itself
no pleasure:

If not possessed, if not enjoyed in thee,
What's earth, or sea, or air, or heaven
    to me?

The highest honors that the world can
    boast,
Are subjects far too low for my desire;
The brightest beams of glory are
    (at most)
But dying sparkles of thy living fire:
The loudest flames that earth can
    kindle, be
But nightly glow-worms, if compared
    to thee.

Without thy presence wealth is bags
    of cares;
Wisdom but folly; joy disquiet—
    sadness;
Friendship is treason, and delights are
    snares;
Pleasures but pains, and mirth but
    pleasing madness;
Without thee, Lord, things be not what
    they be,

Nor have they being, when compared
    with thee.

In having all things, and not thee, what
    have I?
Not having thee, what have my labors
    got?
Let me enjoy but thee, what further
    crave I?
And having thee alone, what have I not?
I wish nor sea nor land; nor would I be
Possessed of heaven, heaven unpossessed
    of thee.

FRANCIS QUARLES
(1591–1644)

Let Me Get Home
Before Dark

For with You is the fountain of life;
in Your light we see light.
PSALM 36:9

*I*t's sundown, Lord.
The shadows of my life stretch back
into the dimness of the years long spent.
I fear not death, for that grim foe
  betrays himself at last,
thrusting me forever into life:
Life with You, unsoiled and free.
But I do fear.
I fear the Dark Spectre may come too
  soon—
or do I mean, too late?
That I should end before I finish or

finish, but not well.
That I should stain Your honor, shame
    Your name,
grieve Your loving heart.
Few, they tell me, finish well. . . .
Lord, let me get home before dark.

The darkness of a spirit
grown mean and small, fruit shriveled
    on the vine,
bitter to the taste of my companions,
burden to be borne by those brave few
    who love me still.
No, Lord. Let the fruit grow lush and
    sweet,
a joy to all who taste;
Spirit-sign of God at work,
stronger, fuller, brighter at the end.
Lord, let me get home before dark.

The darkness of tattered gifts,
rust-locked, half-spent or ill-spent,
a life that once was used of God
    now set aside.
Grief for glories gone or fretting for a

task God never gave.
Mourning in the hollow chambers of
memory,
gazing on the faded banners of victories
long gone.
Cannot I run well unto the end?
Lord, let me get home before dark.

The outer me decays.
I do not fret or ask reprieve.
The ebbing strength but weans me from
mother earth
and grows me up for heaven.
I do not cling to shadows cast by
immortality.
I do not patch the scaffold lent to build
the real, eternal me.
I do not clutch about me my cocoon,
vainly struggling to hold hostage
a free spirit pressing to be born.

But will I reach the gate
in lingering pain, body distorted,
grotesque?

Or will it be a mind
wandering untethered among light
    phantasies or grim terrors?
Of your grace, Father, I humbly ask. . . .
Let me get home before dark.

ROBERTSON MCQUILKIN[9]

SOMETIMES A LIGHT SURPRISES

"As your days, so shall your strength be."
DEUTERONOMY 33:25

Sometimes a light surprises
The Christian while he sings;
It is the Lord, who rises
With healing in His wings.
When comforts are declining,
He grants the soul again
A season of clear shining,
To cheer it after rain.

In holy contemplation,
We sweetly then pursue
The theme of God's salvation,

And find it ever new;
Set free from present sorrow,
We cheerfully can say,
E'en let the unknown to-morrow
Bring with it what it may!

It can bring with it nothing
But He will bear us through;
Who gives the lilies clothing
Will clothe His people too.
Beneath the spreading heavens,
No creature but is fed,
And he who feeds the ravens
Will give His children bread.

The vine nor fig-tree neither
Their wonted fruit should bear,
Though all the fields should wither,
Nor flocks nor herds be there:
Yet God the same abiding
His praise shall tune my voice,
For, while in Him confiding,
I cannot but rejoice.

WILLIAM COWPER
(1731–1800)

RECALLING HIS MERCIES

This I recall to my mind,
Therefore I have hope.
LAMENTATIONS 3:21

Hail, tranquil hour of closing day!
Begone disturbing care!
And look, my soul, from earth away
To Him who heareth prayer.

How sweet the tear of penitence,
Before His throne of grace;
While to the contrite spirit's sense,
He shows His smiling face.

How sweet through long-remembered
    years
His mercies to recall,

And pressed with wants, and griefs, and
    fears,
To trust His love for all.

How sweet to look in thoughtful hope
Beyond the fading sky,
And hear Him call His children up
To His fair home on high.

Calmly the day forsakes our heaven
To dawn beyond the west;
So let my soul in Life's last even
Retire to glorious rest.

LEONARD BACON
(1802–1881)

WE SHOULD REMEMBER

Now may the God of hope fill you with
all joy and peace in believing.
ROMANS 15:13

We should remember our past lost condition, to keep us humble and faithful. We should remember our past failures and mistakes, that we may not repeat them. We should remember past mercies, that we may have confidence in new deeds or trials in the future. We should remember past comforts, that there may be stars in our sky when night comes again.

But while there are these true uses of memory, we should guard against living in the past. We should draw our life inspirations, not from memory, but from hope; not from what is gone, but from what is yet to come. Forgetting the things which are behind, we should reach forward unto those things which are before.

J. R. MILLER

They Also Serve. . .

Rest in the LORD,
and wait patiently for Him.
PSALM 37:7

*W*hen I consider how my light is
    spent,
Ere half my days, in this dark world
    and wide,
And that one talent which is death to
    hide,
Lodged with me useless, though my
    soul more bent
To serve therewith my maker, and
    present
My true account, lest he returning
    chide,

"Doth God exact day-labor, light
  denied,"
I fondly ask; But patience to prevent
That murmur, soon replies, "God doth
  not need
Either man's work or his own gifts, who
  best
Bear his mild yoke, they serve him best,
  his state
Is kingly. Thousands at his bidding
  speed
And post o'er land and ocean without
  rest:
They also serve who only stand and
  wait."

JOHN MILTON
(1608–1674)

I'll Trust in Thee

Trust in the LORD with all your heart.
PROVERBS 3:5

*O*h, friend, are you grieving today because God has refused to give you that which you desired so much? Have you asked Him for something, and it has not been given to you? Then believe Him that His plan is best. Remember that if we ask anything according to His will it shall be given. Then trust Him and rest in His wise decision. When you do that, you will be able to say:

> I will not doubt though all my ships
>   at sea
> Come sailing home with tattered mast
>   and sail;

I will believe the hand that cannot fail
From seeming evil worketh good for me;
And though I weep because those sails
    are tattered,
I still shall cry while my last hope lies
    shattered,
"I'll trust in Thee."
I will not doubt though all my prayers
    return
Unanswered from the still white realm
    above;

I will believe it was an all-wise love
That has refused these things for which
    I yearn;
And though at times I cannot keep
    from grieving,
Still the pure ardor of my fixed believing
Undimmed shall burn.
I will not doubt though sorrows fall like
    rain
And troubles swarm like bees about a
    hive;
I will believe the heights for which I
    strive

Are only reached through anguish and
    through pain;
And though I writhe and groan beneath
    my crosses,
I still shall reap through my severest
    losses,
The greater gain.
I will not doubt; well anchored in this
    faith,
Like some staunch ship my soul braves
    every gale;
So strong its courage that it will not
    quail
To meet the mighty unknown sea of
    death.
Oh, may I cry while body parts with
    spirit,
"I will not doubt," so listening worlds
    may hear it,
With my last breath.

Author Unknown

The Light of
the Spiritual Life

He leads me beside the still waters.
Psalm 23:2

His face was so sad that his little child gently put her hand in his, and said, "Close your eyes, father, and let me lead you." To humor her, he did so, and she led him far away, far from that scene of pain with its sad retrospect, until, coming to a mossy bank by the side of a stream that murmured all day long, she bade him be seated and open his eyes.

And behold, it was the road of all roads sacred to his early love, to the beauty that becalmed his spirit and turned his ambition into its rightful groove, sacred to a mutual promise faithfully kept, to a ministry that never waxed cold. The birds were singing his marriage song again, and the stream whispered of a peace that passeth not away.

Would it not be well if the child of faith would lead us thus? Away from the distraction and tumult, away from the purposeless brooding, unto the realms that are lit with the light of the spiritual life, where every purpose and desire, every duty and relationship,

> *"And every virtue we possess,*
> *And every thought of holiness,"*
> *are trembling with the life Divine.*

What does it mean save this when we say that all things work together for good to them that love Him, than that the future is greater than the past, and hope in every circumstance is winged with richer blessings than memory can ever bear?

Christian Age

I Wish You. . .

*But grow in the grace and knowledge of our
Lord and Savior Jesus Christ.*

2 PETER 3:18

I wish you
some new love
of lovely things,
and some new forgetfulness
of the teasing things,
and some higher pride
in the praising things,
and some sweeter peace
from the hurrying things,
and some closer fence
from the worrying things.

JOHN RUSKIN
(1819–1900)

GOD KNOWS

Therefore the LORD will wait,
that He may be gracious to you.
ISAIAH 30:18

Who knows? God knows: and what
   He knows
Is well and best.
The darkness hideth not from Him,
   but glows
Clear as the morning or the evening
   rose
Of east or west.

Wherefore man's strength is to sit
   still:
Not wasting care
To antedate tomorrow's good or ill;

Yet watching meekly, watching with
    good will,
Watching to prayer.

Christina G. Rossetti
(1830–1894)

It Is a Beauteous Evening

For You are with me.
PSALM 23:4

It is a beauteous evening, calm and
free,
The holy time is quiet as a Nun
Breathless with adoration; the broad sun
Is sinking down in its tranquillity;
The gentleness of heaven broods o'er the
Sea:
Listen! the mighty Being is awake,
And doth with his eternal motion make
A sound like thunder—everlastingly.
Dear Child! dear Girl! that walkest with
me here,
If thou appear untouched by solemn
thought,

Thy nature is not therefore less divine:
Thou liest in Abraham's bosom all the
    year;
And worshipp'st at the Temple's inner
    shrine,
God being with thee when we know
    it not.

William Wordsworth
(1770–1850)

THE SECRET THINGS

Blessed are those
who have not seen
and yet have believed.
JOHN 20:29

The secret things belong to God.
    And so, since it was meant
That faith should soar while reason gropes,
    I've learned to be content.

The things which are revealed belong
    To man. I busy me
With truth this finite mind can grasp
    And leave the rest to Thee.

Blessed are they who, seeing not,
    Yet have believed. Dear Lord,

I give this restless mind to Thee
And take Thee at Thy word!

MARTHA SNELL NICHOLSON

CALLED. . .HELD. . .KEPT

Those whom You gave me I have kept; and none of them is lost.
JOHN 17:12

Just before she died, hymn writer Frances Ridley Havergal asked a friend to read Isaiah 42. Halfway through verse 6, which reads, "I, the LORD, have called You in righteousness, and will hold Your hand: I will keep You," Miss Havergal stopped her friend: "Called, held, kept," she whispered, "That's enough, I'll just go home to glory on those words."

A few minutes later she entered the presence of the Lord. Although Isaiah 42:6 refers to Christ, when Miss Havergal applied them to herself, she expressed her confidence in God to keep her safe until the very end.

CONTENT AND DISCONTENT

I have learned in whatever state I am,
to be content.
PHILIPPIANS 4:11

Some murmur, when their sky is clear
And wholly bright to view,
If one small speck of dark appear
In their great heaven of blue.
And some with thankful love are filled,
If but one streak of light,
One ray of God's good mercy gild
The darkness of their night.

In palaces are hearts that ask,
In discontent and pride,
Why life is such a dreary task,
And all good things denied.

And hearts in poorest huts admire
How Love has in their aid
(Love that not ever seems to tire)
Such rich provision made.

Thou cam'st not to thy place by
    accident,
It is the very place God meant for
    thee;
And should'st thou there small scope
    for action see,
Do not for this give room to
    discontent;
Nor let the time thou owest to God
    be spent
In idly dreaming how thou might-
    est be,
Thy need of grace to help is free.

RICHARD C. TRENCH
(1807–1886)

LIBERTY OF HEART

And you shall know the truth,
and the truth shall make you free.
JOHN 8:32

*B*ut there is yet a liberty of heart
    unsung
By poets, and by senators unpraised,
Which monarchs can not grant, nor
    all the powers
Of earth and hell confederate take
    away:
A liberty, which persecution, fraud,
Oppression, prisons, have no power
    to bind;
Which whoso tastes can be enslaved
    no more.

'Tis liberty of heart, derived from
    heaven;
Bought with His blood who gave it
    to mankind,
And sealed with the same token! It is
    held
By charter, and that charter sanc-
    tioned sure
By the unimpeachable and awful
    oath
And promise of God! His other gifts
All bear the royal stamp that speaks
    them His,
And are august; but this transcends
    them all.

WILLIAM COWPER
(1731–1800)

Peace Is the Pillow for My Head

I will both lie down in peace, and sleep; for You alone, O LORD, make me dwell in safety.
PSALM 4:8

Thus far the Lord has led me on,
Thus far His power prolongs my days;
And every evening shall make known
Some fresh memorial of His grace.

Much of my time has run to waste,
And I perhaps am near my home;
But He forgives my follies past,
He gives me strength for days to come.

I lay my body down to sleep,

Peace is the pillow for my head,
While well-appointed angels keep
Their watchful stations round my bed.

Isaac Watts
(1674–1748)

CONTENTMENT

Now godliness with contentment is great gain.
1 TIMOTHY 6:6

My mind to me a kingdom is;
Such perfect joy therein I find,
As far exceeds all earthly bliss
That world affords, or grows by kind:
Though much I want what most men
        have
Yet doth my mind forbid me crave.

Content I live—this is my stay;
I seek no more than may suffice—
I press to bear no haughty sway;
Look—what I lack my mind supplies.
Lo! thus I triumph like a king,
Content with that my mind doth bring.

Some have too much, yet still they
    crave;
I little have, yet seek no more;
They are but poor—though much they
    have,
And I am rich—with little store.
They poor, I rich: they beg, I give:
They lack, I lend: they pine, I live.

ANCIENT SONG

THE ANCIENT ONE

*Surely goodness and mercy shall follow me all
the days of my life; and I will dwell in the
house of the LORD forever.*
PSALM 23:6

*H*e is insensibly subdued
To settled quiet. He is one by whom
All effort seems forgotten; one to
  whom
Long patience hath such mild com-
  posure given,
That patience now doth seem a
  thing of which
He hath no need. He is by Nature
  led
To peace so perfect, that the young
  behold

With envy what the old man hardly
   feels.

William Wordsworth
(1770–1850)

This story has been translated from the German of Jean Paul Richter's memoir of Fibel,
author of the Bienenroda Spelling Book. It
describes the golden years in the mellow sunset glow of a pure and tranquil life.

The stream of Fibel's history having vanished
under ground, like a second river Rhone, I
was obliged to explore where story or stream
again burst forth, and for this purpose I ques-
tioned every one.

I was told that no one could better
inform me than an exceedingly aged man,
more than a hundred and twenty-five years
old, who lived a few miles from the village of
Bienenroda, and who, having been young at
the same time with Fibel, must know all
about him.

The prospect of shaking hands with the

very oldest man living on the face of the earth enraptured me. I said to myself that a most novel and peculiar sensation must be excited by having a whole past century before you, bodily present, compact and alive, in the century now passing; by holding, hand to hand, a man of the age of the antediluvians, over whose head so many entire generations of young mornings and old evenings have fled, and before whom one stands, in fact, as neither young nor old; to listen to a human spirit, outlandish, behind the time, almost mysteriously awesome; sole survivor of a thousand gray, cold sleepers, coevals of his own remote, hoary age; standing as sentinel before the ancient dead, looking coldly and strangely on life's silly novelties; finding in the present no cooling for his inborn spirit-thirst, no more enchanting yesterdays or tomorrows, but only the day-before-yesterday of youth and the day-after-tomorrow of death.

It may, consequently, be imagined that so very old a man would speak only of the farthest past, of his early day-dawn, which, of course, in the long evening of his protracted day, must now be blending with his midnight.

On the other hand, that one like myself would not feel particularly younger before such a millionaire of hours as Bienenroda Patriarch must be, and that his presence must make one feel more conscious of death than of immortality. A very aged man is a more powerful memento than a grave, for the older a grave is the further we look back to the succession of young persons who have moldered in it; sometimes a maiden is concealed in an ancient grave, but an ancient dwindled body hides only an imprisoned spirit.

An opportunity for visiting the Ancient One was presented by a return coach-and-six, belonging to a count, on which I was admitted to a seat with the coachman. Just before arriving at Bienenroda, he pointed with his whip toward an orchard, tuneful with song, and said: "There sits the old man, with his little animals around him."

I sprang from the noble equipage, and went toward him. I ventured to expect that the count's six horses would give me, before the old man, the appearance of a person of rank, apart from the simplicity of my dress, whereby princes and heroes are wont to distinguish themselves from their tinseled lackeys. I was, therefore, a little surprised that the old man kept on playing with his pet hare, not even checking the barking of his poodle, as if counts were his daily bread, until, at last, he lifted his oilcloth hat from his head. A buttoned overcoat, which gave room to see his vest, a long pair of knit overalls, which were, in fact, enormous stockings, and a neckerchief which hung down to his bosom, made his dress look modern enough.

His timeworn frame was far more peculiar. The inner part of the eye, which is black in childhood, was quite white; his tallness, more than his years, seemed to bow him over into an arch; the outturned point of his chin gave to his speech the appearance of mumbling; yet the expression of his countenance was lively, his eyes bright, his jaws full of white teeth, and his head covered with light hair.

I began by saying: "I came here solely on

your account, to see a man for whom there can, assuredly, be little new under the sun, though he himself is something very new under it. You are now strictly in your five-and-twenties, since, after a century, a new reckoning commences.

"For myself, I confess, after once clambering over the century terminus, or church-wall, of a hundred years, I should neither know how old I was, nor whether I was myself. I should begin fresh and free, just as the world's history has often done, counting again from the year one, in the middle of a thousand years. Yet, why can not a man live to be as old as many a giant tree of India, still standing? It is well to question very old people concerning the methods by which they have prolonged their lives. How do you account for it, dear old sir?"

I was beginning to be vexed at the good man's silence, when he softly replied: "Some suppose it is because I have always been cheerful, because I have adopted the maxim, 'Never sad, ever glad'; but I ascribe it wholly to our dear Lord God, since the animals which here surround us, though never sad, but happy for the most part, by no means so frequently exceed the usual boundary of their life, as does man. He exhibits an image of the eternal God, even in the length of his duration."

Such words concerning God, uttered by a tongue one hundred and twenty-five years old, had great weight and consolation, and I at once felt their beautiful attraction.

On mentioning animals, the old man turned again to his own, and, as though indifferent to him who had come in a coach-and-six, he began again to play with his menagerie—the hare, the spaniel, the silky poodle, the starling, and a couple of turtle-doves on his bosom.

A pleasant bee colony in the orchard also gave heed to him; with one whistle he sent the bees away, and with another he summoned them into the ring of creatures which surrounded him like a court-circle.

At last, he said: "No one need be surprised that a very old man, who has forgotten everything, and whom no one but the dear God knows or cares for should give himself wholly to the dear animals. To whom can such an old man be of much use? I wander about in the villages, as in cities, wholly strange. If I see children, they come before me like my own remote childhood. If I meet old men, they seem like my past hoary years. I do not quite know where I now belong. I hang between heaven and earth.

"Yet God ever looks upon me bright and lovingly, with his two eyes, the sun and the moon. Moreover, animals lead into no sin, but rather to devotion. When my turtle-doves brood over their young and feed them, it seems to me just as if I saw God Himself doing a great deal, for they derive their love and instinct toward their young as a gift from Him."

The old man became silent, and looked pensively before him, as was his inclination. A ringing of christening bells sounded from Bienenroda among the trees in the garden.

He wept a little.

I know not how I could have been so simple, after the beautiful words he had uttered, as to have mistaken his tears for a sign of weakness in his eyes.

"I do not hear well, on account of my great age," he said, "and it seems to me as if the baptismal bell from the distant sanctuary sounded up here very faintly. The old years of my childhood, more than a hundred years ago, ascend from the ancient depths of time, and gaze on me in wonder, while I and they know not whether we ought to weep or laugh."

Then, addressing his silky poodle, he called out, "Ho! ho! come here old fellow!"

The allusion to his childhood brought me to the purpose of my visit. "Excellent sir," said I, "I am preparing the biography of the deceased Master Gotthelf Fibel, author of the famous Spelling Book, and all I now need to complete it is the account of his death."

The old man smiled, and made a low bow.

I continued: "No one is more likely to know the particulars of his decease than yourself, and you are the only person who can enrich me with the rare traits of his childhood, because every incident inscribed on a child's brain grows deeper with years, like names cut into a gourd, while later inscriptions disappear. Tell me, I pray you, all that you know concerning the departed man, for I am to publish his life at the Michaelmas Fair."

He murmured: "Excellent genius, scholar, man of letters, author most famous—these and other fine titles I learned by heart and applied to myself while I was that vain, blinded Fibel, who wrote and published the ordinary spelling book in question."

So, then, this old man was the blessed Fibel himself!

A hundred and twenty-five notes of admiration, ay, eighteen hundred and eleven notes in a row, would but feebly express my astonishment.

[Then followed a long conversation concerning Fibel, after which the narrative continues, as follows:]

The old man went into his little garden-house, and I followed him. He whistled, and instantly a black squirrel came down from a tree, whither it had gone more for pleasure

than for food. Nightingales, thrushes, star-
lings, and other birds flew back into the
open window from the tops of the trees. A
bullfinch, whose color had been changed by
age from red to black, strutted about the
room, uttering droll sounds, which it could
not make distinct. The hare pattered about
in the twilight, sometimes on his hind feet,
sometimes on all fours. Every dog in the
house bounded forward in glad, loving,
human glee.

But the most joyful of all was the poodle;
for he knew he was to have a box, with com-
partments, fastened on his neck, containing
a list of the articles wanted for supper, which
it was his business to bring from the inn in
Bienenroda. He was Fibel's victualer, or pro-
vision-wagon. Children, who ran back and
forth, were the only other ones who minis-
tered to his wants.

In allusion to his pets, he said: "We
ought to assist the circumscribed faculties of
animals by educating them, as far as we can,
since we stand toward them, in a certain
degree as their Lord God; and we ought to

train them to good morals. God and the animals are always good, but not so with man."

Aged men impart spiritual things, as they give material things, with a shaking hand, which drops half. In the effort to gather up his recollections, he permitted me to quicken his memory with my own, and thus I obtained a connected account of some particulars in his experience. He said he might have been about a hundred years old when he cut a new set of teeth, the pain of which disturbed him with wild dreams.

One night he seemed to be holding in his hand a large sieve, and it was his task to pull the meshes apart, one by one. The close network, and the fastening of the wooden rim gave him indescribable trouble. But as his dream went on, he seemed to hold in his hand the great bright sun, which flamed up into his face. He woke with a newborn feeling, and slumbered again as if lying on waving tulips. He dreamed, again, that he was a hundred years old, and that he died as an innocent yearling child, without any of the sin and woe of earth; that he found his parents on high, who brought before him a long procession of his children, who had remained invisible to him while he was in this world, because they were transparent, like the angels. He rose from his bed with new teeth and new ideas.

The old Fibel was consumed, and a true phoenix stood in his place, sunning its colored wings. He had risen glorified, out of no other grave than his own body. The world retreated; heaven came down.

When he had related these things, he at once bade me good-night. Without waiting for the return of his ministering poodle, and with hands folded for prayer, he showed me the road.

I withdrew, but I rambled a long time round the orchard, which had sprung entirely from seed of his own planting. Indeed, he seldom ate a cherry without smuggling the stone and burying it in the ground for a resurrection. This habit often annoyed the neighboring peasants, who did not want high things growing on their boundaries. "But," said he, "I can not destroy a fruit-stone. If the peasants pull up a tree it produces, it will still have lived a little while, and die as a child dies."

While loitering in the orchard, I heard an evening hymn played and sung. I returned near Fibel's window, and saw him slowly turning a hand-organ, and accompanying the tune by softly singing an evening hymn. This organ, aided by a fragment of a voice, sufficed, in its monotonous uniformity, for his domestic devotion. I went away repeating the song, which was written by a Mrs. Browne,

I love to steal awhile away
    From every cumbering care,
And spend the hour of setting day
    In humble grateful prayer.

I love in solitude to shed
    The penitential tear,
And all His promises to plead,
    When none but God is near.

I love to think on mercies past,
    And future good implore;

And all my cares and sorrows cast
    On Him whom I adore.

I love by faith to take a view
    Of brighter scenes in Heaven;
The prospect doth my strength renew,
    While here by tempests driven.

And when life's toilsome day is o'er,
    May its departing ray
Be calm as this impressive hour,
    And lead to endless day.

Beautiful was the orchard when I returned the next morning. And the hoarfrost
of age seemed thawed and fluid and to glisten
only as morning dew on Fibel's after-blossom.
The affection of his animals toward him ren-
dered the morning still more beautiful in an
orchard every tree of which had for its mother
the stone of some fruit that he had enjoyed.
His animals were an inheritance from his parents, though, of course, they were the great,
great, great grandchildren of those which had
belonged to them.

The trees were full of brooding birds, and by a slight whistle he could lure down to his shoulders this tame posterity of his father's singing-school. It was refreshing to the heart to see how quickly the tender flutterers surrounded him.

With the infantile satisfaction of a gray-headed child, he was accustomed to hang up on sticks, or in the trees, wherever the rays of the sun could best shine upon them, little balls of colored glass; and he took indescribable delight in this accordion of silver, gold, and jewel hues.

These parti-colored sun-balls, varying the green with many flaming tints, were like crystal tulip-beds. Some of the red ones seemed like ripe apples among the branches. But what charmed the old man most were reflections from the landscape from these little world-spheres. They resembled the moving prospects shadowed forth in a diminishing mirror. "Ah," said he, "when I contemplate the colors produced by the sunshine which God gives to this dark world, it seems to me as if I had departed, and were already with

God. And yet, since He is in us, we are always with God."

I asked him how it happened that, at his age, he spoke German almost purer than that used even by our best writers. Counting his birth from the end of his century (the new birth described in his dream), he replied: "I was somewhere about two years old, when I happened to hear a holy, spiritual minister, who spoke German with such an angel-tongue, that he would not have needed a better in heaven."

He could not tell me the preacher's name, but he vividly described his manner in the pulpit. He told how he spoke with no super-fluity of words, airs, or gestures; how he uttered, in mild tones, things the most beau-tiful and forcible; how, like the apostle John, with his resting-place close to heaven, this man spoke to the world, laying his hands calmly on the pulpit desk as an arm-case; how his every tone was a heart, and his every look a blessing; how the energy of this disciple of Christ was imbedded in love, as the firm dia-mond is encased in the ductile gold; how the pulpit was to him a Mount Tabor, whereon he transfigured both himself and his hearers; and how, of all clergymen, he best performed that which is the most difficult—the praying worthily.

My feelings grew constantly warmer toward this timeworn man, while I did not require a full return of affection from him any more than I should from a little child. But I remembered that I ought not to disturb the evening of his days with things of the world, and that I ought to depart. I would have him preserve, undisturbed, that sublime position of old age, where man lives, as it were, at the pole: where no star rises or sets; where the whole firmament is motionless and clear, while the Pole-star of another world shines fixedly overhead.

I therefore said to him that I would return in the evening and take my leave.

To my surprise, he replied that perhaps he should himself take leave of the whole world at evening, and that he wished not to be disturbed when dying. He said that he should that evening read to the end of the

Revelation of St. John, and perhaps it might be the end with him, also.

I ought to have mentioned previously that he read continually, and read nothing but the Bible, regularly from the beginning to the end; and he had a fixed impression that he should depart on concluding the twentieth and twenty-first verses of the twenty-second chapter of the Revelation of John: "He which testifieth of all things saith, Surely I come quickly: Amen. Even so come, Lord Jesus. The grace of our Lord Jesus Christ be with you all. Amen." In consequence of this belief, he was in the habit of reading the last books of the Bible faster.

Little as I believed in so sudden a withering of his protracted after-blossom, I obeyed his latest-formed wish. Whenever a right wish is expressed by any man, we should do well to remember that it may be his last.

I took my leave, requesting him to intrust me with his testamentary commissions for the village. He said they had been taken charge of long ago, and the children knew them.

He cut a twig from a Christmas tree, coeval in his childhood, and presented me with it as a keepsake.

In the beautiful summer evening, I could not refrain from stealthily approaching the house, through the orchard, to ascertain whether the good old man had ended his Bible and his life together.

On the way, I found the torn envelope of a letter, sealed with a black seal, and over me the white storks were speeding their way to a warmer country. I was not much encouraged when I heard all the birds singing in his orchard, for their ancestors had done the same when his father died.

A towering cloud, full of the latest twilight, spread itself before my shortsighted vision, like a far-off, blooming, foreign landscape; and I could not comprehend how it was that I had never before noticed this strange-looking, reddish land; so much the more easily did it occur to me that this might be his Orient, whither God was leading the weary one. I had become so confused as actually to mistake red bean-blossoms for a bit of fallen sunset. Presently I heard a man singing, to the accompaniment of an organ. It was the ancient one singing his evening hymn:

Lord of my life, another day
Once more hath sped away.

The birds in the room, and those in the distant branches, also, chimed in with his song. The bees, too, joined in with their humming, as in the warm summer evening they dived into the cups of the linden blossoms.

My joy kindled into a flame. He was alive! But I would not disturb his holy evening. I would let him remain with Him who had surrounded him with gifts and with years, and not call upon him to think of any man here below.

I listened to the last verse of his hymn, that I might be still more certain of the actual continuance of his life, and then tardily I slipped away.

To my joy, I still found, in the eternal youth of Nature, beautiful references to his lengthened age; from the everlasting rippling of the brook in the meadow to a late swarm of bees, which had settled themselves on a linden tree, probably in the forenoon, before two o'clock, as if, by taking their lodging with him, he was to be their bee-father, and continue to live. Every star twinkled to me a hope.

I went to the orchard very early in the morning, wishing to look upon the ancient one in sleep—death's angel prelude, the warm dream of cold death. But he was reading, and had read, in his large printed Bible, far beyond the deluge, as I could see by the engravings I held it to be a duty not to interrupt his solitude long. I told him I was going away, and gave him a little farewell billet, instead of farewell words.

I was much moved, though silent.

It was not the kind of emotion with which we take leave of a friend, or a youth, or an old man; it was like parting from a remote stranger-being, who scarcely glances at us from the high, cold clouds which hold him between the earth and the sun. There is a stillness of soul which resembles the stillness of bodies on a frozen sea, or on high mountains; every loud tone is an interruption too prosaically harsh, as in the softest adagio.

Even those words, "for the last time," the old man had long since left behind him. Yet he hastily presented to me my favorite flower, a blue Spanish vetch in an earthen pot. This butterfly flower is the sweeter inasmuch as it so easily exhales its perfume and dies. He said he had not yet sung the usual morning hymn, which followed the service of his death-evening; and he begged me not to take it amiss that he did not accompany me, or once look after me, especially as he could not see very well. He then added, almost with emotion, "O friend, may you live virtuously! We shall meet again, where my departed relatives will be present, and also that great preacher, whose name I have forgotten. We meet again."

He turned immediately, quite tranquilly to his organ. I parted from him as from a life. He played from his organ beneath the trees, and his face was turned toward me; but to his dim eyes I knew that I should soon become a motionless cloud. So I remained till he began his morning hymn, from old Neander:

> *The Lord still leaves me living,*
>   *I hasten him to praise;*
> *My joyful spirit giving,*
>   *He hears my early lays.*

While he was singing, the birds flew round him; the dogs, accustomed to the music, were silent; and it even wafted the swarm of bees into their hive. Bowed down as he was by age, his figure was so tall that, from the distance where I stood, he looked sufficiently erect. I remained until the ancient one had sung the twelfth and last verse of his morning hymn:

> *Ready my cause to finish,*
>   *And come, O God, to Thee;*
> *A conscience pure I cherish,*
>   *Till death shall summon me.*

Human Argument
at Its Best

For the Immortality of the Soul

For now we see in a mirror, dimly, but then face to face. Now I know in part, but then I shall know just as I also am known.
1 Corinthians 13:12

Joseph Addison was a great English essayist who founded *The Spectator* and wrote most of its essays, but he is probably best remembered for his hymns. A graduate of Oxford, he served as a member of Parliament for eleven years. On his deathbed, he sent for a friend whom he hoped to reclaim from a dissipated and licentious life. "I have sent for you," he said, "that you may see in what peace a Christian can die."

Here are some of Addison's thoughts:

How can it enter into the thoughts of man that the soul, which is capable of such immense perfections, and of receiving new improvements to all eternity, shall fall away into nothing almost as soon as it is created? Are such abilities made for no purpose?

An animal arrives at a point of perfection that it can never pass; in a few years it has all the endowments it is capable of; and were it to live ten thousand more, would be the same thing it is at present.

Were a human soul thus at a stand in its accomplishments; were its faculties to be full-blown, and incapable of further enlargements, I could imagine it might fall away insensible, and drop at once into a state of annihilation.

But can we believe a thinking being, that is in a perpetual progress of improvements, and traveling on from perfection to perfection, after having just looked abroad into the works of its Creator, and made few discoveries of His infinite goodness, wisdom, and power, must perish at his first setting out, and in the very beginning of his inquiries?

Man, considered in his present state, seems only sent into the world to propagate his kind. He provides himself with a successor, and immediately quits his post to make room for him. Heir crowds heir, as in a rolling flood. Wave urges wave.

He does not seem born to enjoy life, but to deliver down to others. This is not surprising to consider in animals, which are formed for our use, and can finish their business in a short life. The silkworm, after having spun her task, lays her eggs and dies.

But in this life man can never take in his full measure of knowledge; nor has he time to subdue his passions, establish his soul in virtue, and come up to the perfection of his nature before he is hurried off the stage.

Would an infinitely wise God make such glorious creatures for so mean a purpose? Can He delight in the production of such abortive intelligence, such short-lived reasonable beings? Would He give us talents that are not to be exerted? Capacities that are never to be gratified? How can we find that wisdom which shines through all His works, in the formation of man, without looking on this world as only a nursery for the next, and believing that the several generations of rational creatures, which rise up and disappear in such quick successions, are only to receive their first rudiments of existence here, and afterward to be transplanted into a more friendly climate, where they may spread and flourish to all eternity?

There is not, in my opinion, a more pleasing and triumphant consideration in religion than this of the perpetual progress which the soul makes toward the perfection of its nature, without ever arriving at a period in it! To look upon the soul as going on from strength to strength, to consider that it is to shine forever with new accessions of glory and brighten to all eternity; that it will be still adding virtue to virtue and knowledge to knowledge, carries in it something wonderfully agreeable to that ambition which is natural to the mind of man.

Nay, it must be a prospect pleasing to God Himself to see His creation forever beautifying in His eyes, and drawing nearer to Him by greater degrees of resemblance.

Methinks this single consideration of the progress of a finite spirit to perfection will be sufficient to extinguish all envy in inferior natures, and all contempt in superior. That cherubim, which now appears as a god to a human soul, knows very well that the period will come about in eternity when the human soul shall be as perfect as he himself now is; nay, when it shall look down upon that degree of perfection as much as it now falls short of it.

It is true the higher nature still advances, and by that means preserves his distance and superiority in the scale of being; but he knows that how high soever the station is of which he stands possessed at present, the inferior nature will at length mount up to it, and shine forth in the same degree of glory.

With what astonishment and veneration may we look into our own souls, where there are such hidden stores of virtue and knowledge, such inexhausted sources of perfection!

We know not yet what we shall be, nor will it ever enter into the heart of man to conceive the glory that will be always in reserve for him. The soul, considered in relation to its Creator, is like one of those mathematical lines that may draw nearer to another for all eternity without a possibility of touching it; and can there be a thought so transporting as to consider ourselves in these perpetual approaches to Him who is not only the standard of perfection but of happiness?

When all Thy mercies, O my God,
    My rising soul surveys,
Transported with the view,
    I'm lost in wonder, love and praise.

Unnumbered comforts to my soul
    Thy tender care bestowed,
Before my infant heart conceived
    From whom those comforts flowed.

When worn with sickness, oft hast Thou
    With health renewed my face;

And, when in sins and sorrows bowed,
Revived my soul with grace.

Thru every period of my life
Thy goodness I'll pursue,
And after death, in distant worlds,
The glorious theme renew.

JOSEPH ADDISON
(1672–1719)

THE SANDS OF TIME
ARE SINKING

And they sang a new song, saying,
You are worthy.
REVELATION 5:9

Samuel Rutherford (1600–1661) left us 365 inspiring letters. This piece, by Mrs. A. R. Cousin, originally consisting of nineteen stanzas, has become a household hymn all over the English-speaking world. Many of the lines in the hymn are taken directly from Rutherford's letters. It is recorded that his dying words were, "Glory, glory dwelleth in Immanuel's Land."

The sands of time are sinking,
The dawn of Heaven breaks,

The summer morn I've sighed for,
The fair sweet morn awakes:
Dark, dark hath been the midnight,
But dayspring is at hand,
And glory—glory dwelleth
In Immanuel's land.

The King there in His beauty,
Without a veil, is seen:
It were a well-spent journey,
Though seven deaths lay between.
The Lamb, with His fair army,
Doth on Mount Zion stand,
And glory—glory dwelleth
In Immanuel's land.

With mercy and with judgment
My web of time He wove,
And aye the dews of sorrow
Were lustred with His love.
I'll bless the hand that guided,
I'll bless the heart that plann'd,
When throned where glory dwelleth
In Immanuel's land.

The Bride eyes not her garment,
But her dear Bridegroom's face;
I will not gaze at glory,
But on my King of Grace—
Not at the crown He gifteth,
But on His pierced hand:
The Lamb is all the glory
Of Immanuel's land.

MRS. A. R. COUSIN
(1824–1906)

It Lies Around Us
like a Cloud

We do not look at the things which are seen,
but at the things which are not seen.
2 Corinthians 4:18

*I*t lies around us like a cloud—
A world we do not see;
Yet the sweet closing of an eye
May bring us there to be.

Its gentle breezes fan our cheek,
Amid our worldly cares
Its gentle voices whisper love,
And mingle with our prayers.

To close the eye and close the ear,
Wrapped in a trance of bliss,

And gently drawn in loving arms,
To swoon to that—from this.

Scarce knowing if we wake or sleep,
Scarce asking where we are
To feel all evil slink away,
All sorrow and all care.

Sweet souls around us! watch us still,
Press nearer to our side;
Into our thoughts, into our prayers,
With gentle helpings glide.

Let death between us be as naught,
A dried and vanished stream;
Your joy be the reality,
Our suffering life the dream.

Harriet Beecher Stowe
(1811–1896)

A Psalm About the Shortness of Life

You will guide me with Your counsel,
and afterward receive me to glory.
Psalm 73:24

said
O Lord
let me end the work
You gave to me to do.
So much
must yet be done
before the dark
so little time
remains
before I'm home.
You are eternal

God
a thousand years to You
is but a passing day.
You scatter ages
I hoard my hours.
Please understand
my need for time
to do Your will
complete my job.
I understand
He said
I do.
I only had
three years
of days
and I was through.

JOSEPH BAYLY[10]

My Heart Leaps Up

When I consider Your heavens. . .
PSALM 8:3

My heart leaps up when I behold
A rainbow in the sky:
So was it when my life began;
So is it now I am a man;
So be it when I shall grow old,
Or let me die!
The Child is father of the Man;
And I could wish my days to be
Bound each to each by natural piety.

WILLIAM WORDSWORTH
(1770–1850)

Joy Shall Overtake Us

But may the God of all grace, who called us
to His eternal glory by Christ Jesus,
after you have suffered a while, perfect,
establish, strengthen, and settle you.
1 PETER 5:10

Fly envious time, till thou run out
    thy race,
Call on the lazy leaden-stepping hours,
Whose speed is but the heavy plummet's
    pace;
And glut thyself with what thy womb
    devours,
Which is no more than what is false and
    vain,
And merely mortal dross;
So little is our loss,

So little is thy gain.
For when as each thing bad thou hast
    entombed,
And last of all thy greedy self consumed,
Then long eternity shall greet our bliss
With an individual kiss;
And joy shall overtake us as a flood,
When everything that is sincerely good
And perfectly divine,
With truth, and peace, and love, shall
    ever shine
About the supreme throne
Of Him, to whose happy-making sight
    alone,
When once our heavenly-guided soul
    shall climb.
Then all this earthly grossness quit,
Attired with stars, we shall forever sit,
Triumphing over death, and chance,
    and thee O time.

JOHN MILTON
(1608–1674)

No Wrinkles in My Soul

Now to Him who is able to keep you from
stumbling, and to present you faultless before
the presence of His glory with exceeding joy.
JUDE 1:24

I had my picture taken,
It was clear as it could be,
But wrinkles here and wrinkles there
Were all that I could see—
Dear Lord, I cried, it's all so plain,
The past years took their toll,
But how I pray that I will have
No wrinkles in my soul. . .

Oh take from me my fear and worry,
Iron out all my doubt,
Help me to know that trust is what

My faith is all about. . .
Lord, give me hope through everything,
A spirit brave and strong,
And keep me from depression
When my days are bleak and long—

Oh give me courage that won't fail
And wisdom for my days,
And take from me all bitterness
And fill my heart with praise;
Oh make me kind and loving, Lord,
And always understanding,
And when I think someone is wrong
Keep me from reprimanding;

Please take from me all useless grieving
When my life seems cold—
Now I don't mind the facial wrinkles,
But when You call the roll
I'd like to stand before You
With no wrinkles in my soul.

AUTHOR UNKNOWN

An "Envelope"—
the Immediate Body

For in this we groan,
earnestly desiring to be clothed with our
habitation which is from heaven.
2 Corinthians 5:2

In these few verses—2 Corinthians 5:1–8
—we have some of the most precious disclo-
sures in all Scripture of the sequel of the
Christian's death. Let us set out reverently a
few of these guarded and sparing truths.
They concern the beauties of that wonderful
morn when the pilgrim finally strikes his tent
and moves into his eternal home.

1. At death the spirit leaves the mortal
   body. The conscious self is "absent

from the body" or "leaves its home
in the body." Between death and resurrection that connection is broken.
But we are not to assume for certain
that the outgoer is therefore form-
less, bodiless. It may be that the pas-
sage we have covered teaches that an
"envelope" will be provided at once
for the soul, and we incline to think
that it does. In that case the body of
the resurrection will be, so to speak,
the efflorescence of that envelope
and continuous with it and with the
present body, by the identity of the
wearer, the subject. We dare not pro-
nounce with certainty. But the
angels have power to "materialize" a
bodily vehicle. So the human spirit,
yonder, may well have a similar privilege, the possession of an organ for
its life and action, pending the resurrection glory.

2. That beyond the veil light reigns we
are to be quite sure. Whittier is true

to revelation when he says that

Death is a covered way which opens into light.

It is a tunnel, a very short tunnel, with a summer landscape at the far end. On the outside of the tunnel the whole day is shining all the while. And the day is breaking already, from the end, into the darkness underneath the roof.

Wonderful visions have been given of that light, now and then to passing souls. A Scottish believer, strong, self-restrained, a characteristic son of the Presbyterian Church, Dr. Kalley, approached his end, an aged man. As a veteran medical practitioner, he calmly told his wife how he must expect to die suddenly, but that he hoped to give her notice. One day he laid his hand on her arm, said the words, "Oh, my dear wife!" and immediately expired. The words and his manner, said Mrs. Kalley, were precisely those with which, years before, during a tour they took in the Highlands, he touched her arm and bade her look, when suddenly a mountain view of entrancing grandeur broke upon them.

BISHOP HANDLEY C. G. MOULE
(1841–1920)

Joy, Shipmate, Joy

But we know that when He is revealed,
we shall be like Him,
for we shall see Him as He is.
1 John 3:2

And now I am seventy years old, and this gives me permission to stand aloof from the stress of life, and to lay down all burden of responsibility for carrying on the work of the world, and I rejoice in my immunity.

I love Walt Whitman's matchless song,

Joy, shipmate, joy.
(Pleased to the soul at death, I cry.)
Our life is closed, our life begins;
The long, long anchorage we leave
The ship is clear at last, she leaps

She swiftly courses from the shore!
Joy, shipmate, joy!

This passing life with all its affairs, once apparently so important, fades into insignificance in the face of the surpassing life beyond.

I am like the butterfly, just preparing to slip out of its old cocoon, panting for the life outside, but with no experience to tell it what sort of a life that outside life will be. Only I believe with all my heart that the Apostle told the truth when he declared that "eye hath not seen, nor ear heard, neither have entered into the heart of man the things which God hath prepared for them that love Him." And what more delicious prospect could the soul have! I remember vividly my perfect delight many years ago in the prospect of exploring the unknown beauties of the Yellowstone Park, and of the Hoodoo Mountains in Wyoming Territory, a delight caused largely by the fact that they were unknown, and that therefore anything and everything seemed possible. But that delight was as nothing compared to my delight now, in looking forward to the things which have not even entered my mind to conceive.

The one thing I do know about it is, that then will be fulfilled the prayer of our Lord, "Father, I will that they also, whom thou hast given me, be with me where I am; that they may behold my glory, which thou hast given me" (John 17:24 KJV). That glory is not the glory of dazzling light and golden brightness, as some might picture it, but it is the glory of unselfish love, than which there can be no greater. I have had a few faint glimpses of this glory now and here, and it has been enough to ravish my heart. But there I shall see Him as He is, in all the glory of an infinite unselfishness which no heart of man has ever been able to conceive; and I await the moment with joy.

HANNAH WHITALL SMITH
(1832–1911)

The Story of a Dream

And if I go and prepare a place for you,
I will come again and receive you to Myself;
that where I am,
there you may be also.
JOHN 14:3

How gentle God's commands, how
    kind His precepts are!
Come cast your burden on the Lord,
    and trust His constant care
While Providence supports, let saints
    securely dwell;
That hand which bears all nature up
    shall guide His children well
His goodness stands approved down to
    the present day

I'll drop my burden at His feet and bear
a song away.

PHILIP DODDRIDGE
(1702–1751)

Dr. Philip Doddridge of Northampton, England, the celebrated author of the New Testament commentary, spent many happy hours in fellowship with Dr. Samuel Clarke, an intimate friend. A favorite topic of conversation was the intermediate state of the soul. They believed that at the instant of death the soul was not immediately introduced into the presence of all the heavenly host, nor into the full glory of the heavenly state.

One evening, after a conversation of this nature, Dr. Doddridge retired to rest with his mind still full of the subject. In "the visions of the night," while the eyes of the body were closed in sleep, he passed into another life, in a certain sense, and by another power, as yet unknown to mortals, he saw, heard, and acted.

In his dream, he was at the house of his friend, where he was suddenly taken ill. By degrees, he seemed to grow worse and at last to die. In that instant he realized he had passed into another and higher state of existence. He had exchanged a state of mortality and suffering for one of immortality and happiness.

Embodied in an aerial form, he seemed to float in a region of pure light. There was nothing below but the melancholy group of his friends weeping around his lifeless remains. Thrilled with joy, he was surprised at their tears, and he attempted to inform them of his happy change, but by some mysterious power his voice was silent; he rose silently upon the air, and their forms gradually receded from his sight.

While in golden clouds, he found himself swiftly mounting the skies with a venerable figure at his side, guiding his mysterious movements. In his companion's face he observed youth and old age blended together with an intimate harmony and majestic sweetness. He and this figure traveled together through a vast space, until at length the towers of a glorious building appeared in the distance. As its form arose brilliant and distinct among the far-off shadows across their path, the guide informed him that the palace he beheld was to be for the present his mansion of rest.

They soon reached the door, where they entered. The guide introduced him into a spacious apartment, at the end of which stood a table, covered with a snow-white cloth, a golden cup, and a cluster of grapes. The guide then said he must now leave him, but that Doddridge must remain, for he would receive, in a short time, a visit from the Lord of the mansion. During the interval before his arrival the apartment would furnish Doddridge with sufficient entertainment and instruction.

The guide vanished, and Doddridge was left alone. He began to examine the decorations of the room and observed that the walls were adorned with a number of pictures. Upon closer inspection he found, to his astonishment, that they formed a complete biography of his own life. Here he saw upon the canvas that angels, though unseen, had ever been his familiar attendants; sent by God, they had sometimes preserved him from imminent peril. He beheld himself first as an infant almost dying, when his life was prolonged by an angel breathing into his nostrils. Most of the occurrences were perfectly familiar to his recollection, but they unfolded many things he had never before understood, which had perplexed him with many doubts and much uneasiness.

He was particularly struck with a picture in which he was represented as falling from his horse, when death would have been inevitable had not an angel received him in his arms and broken the force of his fall. These proofs of God's mercy filled him with joy and gratitude, and his heart overflowed with love as he surveyed in them all an exhibition of goodness and love far beyond all he had imagined.

Suddenly, his attention was arrested by a rap at the door—the Lord of the mansion had arrived. The door opened and He entered. So powerful and so overwhelming, and of such singular beauty was His appearance, that Doddridge sank down at His feet completely overcome by His majestic appearance. His Lord gently raised him from the ground, and, taking him by the hand, led him forward to the table. The Lord pressed with His finger the juice of grapes into the golden cup, and after He had Himself drunk, He presented it to Doddridge, saying: "This is the new wine in my Father's kingdom." No sooner had Doddridge partaken than all uneasy sensation vanished; perfect love had cast out fear, and he conversed with his Savior as an intimate friend. Like the silver rippling of a summer sea, he heard from His lips these words, "Thy labors are over, thy work is approved; rich and glorious is the reward."

Thrilled with an unspeakable bliss that glided over his spirit and slid into the very depths of his soul, he suddenly saw glories upon glories bursting upon his view.

Then he awoke.

Tears of rapture from his joyful interview were rolling down his cheeks. The vivid impression of his dream remained in his mind for a long time, and he could never speak of it without great joy and tenderness.

We Shall Be like Him

Behold what manner of love
The Father has bestowed on us,
That we should be called children of
    God!
Therefore the world does not know us,
Because it did not know Him.

Beloved, now we are children of God;
And it has not yet been revealed
What we shall be,
But we know that when He is revealed,
We shall be like Him,
For we shall see Him as He is.

1 John 3:1–2

The German poet von Goethe (1749–1832) stood one day with his friend Johann

Peter Eckermann (1792–1854), on Weimar road, at a point from which the outlook was simply majestic. Together they gazed in rapt attention at the setting sun. The great poet and philosopher tremulously exclaimed: "Setting, nevertheless the sun is always the same sun. I am fully convinced that our spirit is a being of a nature quite indestructible, and that its activity continues from eternity to eternity."

The soul may set—it may go down into the unseen realm; nevertheless it is always the same "indestructible" soul!

It Grows More Real Day by Day

In My Father's house are many mansions;
if it were not so, I would have told you.
I go to prepare a place for you.
JOHN 14:2

*L*ife changes all our thoughts of
    heaven;
At first we think of streets of gold,
Of gates of pearl and dazzling light,
Of shining wings and robes of white,
And things all strange to mortal sight.

But in the afterward of years
It is a more familiar place;
A *home* unhurt by sighs or tears,
Where waiteth many a well-known face.

With passing months it comes more
    near,
It grows more real day by day;
Not strange or cold, but very dear—
The glad *homeland* not far away,
Where none are sick, or poor, or lone,
The place where we shall find our own.

And as we think of all we knew
Who there have met to part no more,
Our longing hearts desire home too,
With all the strife and trouble o'er.

ROBERT BROWNING
(1812–1889)

THANKS

Giving thanks always for all things.
EPHESIANS 5:20

Thanks to God for my Redeemer,
Thanks for all Thou dost provide!
Thanks for times now but a mem'ry,
Thanks for Jesus by my side!
Thanks for pleasure, balmy springtime,
Thanks for dark and dreary fall!
Thanks for tears by now forgotten,
Thanks for peace within my soul!

Thanks for prayers that Thou hast
    answered,
Thanks for what Thou dost deny!
Thanks for storms that I have weathered,
Thanks for all Thou dost supply!

Thanks for pain, and thanks for pleasure,
Thanks for comfort in despair!
Thanks for grace that none can measure,
Thanks for love beyond compare!

Thanks for roses by the wayside,
Thanks for thorns their stems contain!
Thanks for home and thanks for fireside,
Thanks for hope, the sweet refrain!
Thanks for joy and thanks for sorrow,
Thanks for heav'nly peace with Thee!
Thanks for hope in the tomorrow,
Thanks thro' all eternity!

Unknown

THE WAY IN

I am the way.
JOHN 14:6

*D*uring the tragic war between the states, a young soldier in the Union Army lost his older brother and his father in the battle of Gettysburg. The soldier went to Washington, D.C., to see President Lincoln about an exemption from military service so he could go home and help his sister with the spring planting on the farm.

When he approached the front gate he was quickly brushed aside by the guards on duty. "The President is a very busy man! Now go back out there on the battle lines where you belong."

Disheartened, the soldier sat down on a

park bench not far from the White House. A little boy came up to him and said, "Soldier, you look unhappy. What's wrong?" The soldier looked up at the little boy and spilled out his heart to him.

"I can help you, soldier," the young lad said. He took the soldier by the hand and led him straight back to the White House, past all the guards. After they got inside, they walked past the generals and high-ranking officials. Finally, they reached the Oval Office—where the President was working—and the little boy didn't even knock on the door. He just walked right in and led the soldier with him. There behind the desk was President Abraham Lincoln and his secretary of state, looking over battle plans that were laid out on the desk.

The president looked first at the boy and then at the soldier and said, "Good afternoon, Todd, will you introduce me to your friend?" And Todd Lincoln, the son of the president said, "Daddy, this soldier needs to talk to you, for it seems that only you can help him."

The soldier pleaded his case before Mr. Lincoln, and right then and there he received the exemption that he desired.

But how may a person get to heaven?

My friends, there is only one mediator between God and men. It is the Lord Jesus Christ, who gave Himself a ransom for us all (1 Timothy 2:5–6). No one can come to the Father in heaven but by Him, Christ Jesus, the mediator who died for our sins. "But now in Christ Jesus you who once were far off have been brought near by the blood of Christ. . . . For through Him we both have access by one Spirit to the Father" (Ephesians 2:13, 18).

So frequently people are urged to do something, instead of being invited to receive that which God has already provided in the finished work of Christ as mediator.

Campbell Murray, who was an office holder in the Scottish kirk for some fifty years, was reading a magazine article when he noticed the words: "The gospel brings to us not a work to do, but a word to believe about a work already done." The glorious truth of Christ's finished work dawned upon his mind, and with considerable excitement he called to his wife and said, "I believe it, I believe it; I have been working at the keyhole all these years while the door of salvation has been open all the time."

Indeed the door of salvation is wide open! Perfect righteousness is available unto all, and upon all them that believe (Romans 3:22).

Are you saved? There is nothing you can give to God to be saved. There is nothing you can do to be saved. The work of salvation has been completed. Jesus is ready and willing to save you right now. Will you just believe in Him, believe His Word, and pass from death unto life (John 5:24)?

> In great love You sought me,
> With your own blood You bought me;
> How can I but trustingly receive You,
> And eternally believe You—
> My Savior! my God!—everlastingly true.

N. A. WOYCHUK

BEYOND THE SUNSET

There shall be no night there.

REVELATION 22:5

A group of Christian friends were gathered at Homer Rodeheaver's home on Rainbow Point on Winona Lake, Indiana, to watch a breathtaking sunset over the lake. Our heavenly Father was slowly drawing the curtains of heaven amid the symphony of breathtaking color, and the friends grasped for words to describe the glory of that sunset. That night at their hillside apartment one couple sat down at the old piano, and wrote these beautiful words and set them to music.

Beyond the sunset, O blissful morning
When with our Saviour heav'n is begun

Earth's toiling ended, O glorious
    dawning;
Beyond the sunset, when day is done

Beyond the sunset no clouds will gather,
No storms will threaten, no fears annoy;
O day of gladness, O day unending,
Beyond the sunset, eternal joy!

Beyond the sunset a hand will guide me
To God, the Father, whom I adore;
His glorious presence, His words of
    welcome,
Will be my portion on that fair shore.

Beyond the sunset, O glad reunion,
With our dear loved ones who've gone
    before;
In that fair homeland we'll know no
    parting,
Beyond the sunset, for evermore!

VIRGIL AND BLANCHE BROCK

Our Ultimate Perfection

- Perfect sinlessness—"And there shall be no more curse."

- Perfect authority—"But the throne of God and of the Lamb shall be in it."

- Perfect obedience—"And His servants shall serve Him."

- Perfect communion—"They shall see His face."

- Perfect consecration—"And His name shall be on their foreheads."

- Perfect blessedness—"There shall be no night there."

- Perfect glory—"And they shall reign forever and ever."

Revelation 22:3–5

DEATH ITSELF SHALL DIE

Then shall be brought to pass
the saying that is written:
"Death is swallowed up in victory."
1 CORINTHIANS 15:54

Lo, what a glorious sight appears
To our believing eyes!
The earth and sea are passed away,
And the old rolling skies.

From the third heaven where God
    resides,
That holy happy place,
The New Jerusalem comes down
Adorn'd with shining grace.

Attending angels shout for joy,
And the bright armies sing,

"Mortals, behold the sacred seat
Of your descending king.

"The God of glory down to men
Removes His blest abode,
Men the dear objects of His grace,
And He the loving God.

"His own soft hand shall wipe the tears
From every weeping eye,
And pains, and groans, and griefs, and
    fears,
And death itself shall die."

ISAAC WATTS
(1674–1748)

How Long the Night

Its gates shall not be shut at all by day (there shall be no night there).
REVELATION 21:25

How long the night? I do not know, and
God in mercy does not show me
How long the night.

How soon the harvest? I can't tell, and
He whose sun and rain will swell the
    seed—He does not say.

How long until? How long to wait?
How long before at Heaven's gate
    will justice come?

Pray, Watchman, say, when comes the
    dawn?
My hope, my faith are nearly gone.
How long the night?

An answer comes now through the shade;
The voice is firm—I am afraid
I've tempted God.

Have I been rash? What will He say?
He speaks, His words my fear allay,
"The day is sure.

"The day is sure, my child beloved,
The darkness covering above you
cannot last.

"Would you could see it from my side,
    it thins; it cannot long abide the light
I pour your way.

"It comes—the Day!
And do not fear the seed won't grow
    beneath the sod where it was sown.
It's growing now.

The harvest comes, it will not wait, tho'
    it seems long, it's growing late,

"I tell you true,
The harvest comes,
I promise you."

O Lord, my eyes can only see the earth-
    side shape of things to be,
And tho' I cry,

I now confess Your Word, my own, and
    fix my heart on You alone,
Who speaks to me.

I say, The Day is sure,
the night will fade, the harvest—tho' it
    seems delayed—will surely come.

My eyes shall see it, all around the light,
    the wheat upon the ground,
When morning comes,
When harvest comes,
My eyes shall see.

EDWARD HENRY JOY
(1871–1949)

THE CITY OF
CELESTIAL HEALTH

And the inhabitant will not say,
"I am sick."
ISAIAH 33:24

City of celestial health,
Into which no sickness comes,
Where, in everlasting wealth,
We shall find our home of homes.
City of the tranquil breast,
Where the heartache is unknown;
Home of softest calm and rest,
Life's long fever past and gone.
There, amid the ransomed blest,
I shall be a welcome guest,—
I, a sinner, yet at rest.

City of the pardoning love,
Dwelling place of the forgiven,
Glory of the land above,
Center of God's holy heaven.
City of the sinless host:
Army upon army see,
Gathered from the countless lost,
Clothed in heavenly purity.
There, amid the ransomed blest,
I shall be a welcome guest,
I, a sinner, yet at rest.

AUTHOR UNKNOWN

CLOTHED WITH IMMORTALITY

This mortal has put on immortality.
1 CORINTHIANS 15:54

Clothed with immortality;
What will it be? What will it be?
A sudden shiver—
Then deathless ever.

Clothed with immortality;
How strange 'twill be! How strange
    'twill be!
A sweet confusion,
Almost illusion!

Clothed with immortality;

How soon 'twill be! How soon 'twill be!
The eyelids fall
Has witnessed all!

Clothed with immortality;
When will it be? When will it be?
Haste, dear Lord Jesus;
From death release us.

WATCHWORD

WHAT IS THIS SPLENDOR?

Your eyes will see the King in His beauty; they
will see the land that is very far off.
ISAIAH 33:17

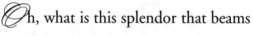h, what is this splendor that beams
   on me now,
This beautiful sunrise that dawns on my
   soul,
While faint and far-off land and sea lie
   below,
And under my feet the huge golden
   clouds roll?

To what mighty king doth this city
   belong,
With its rich jeweled shrines and its
   gardens of flowers,

With its breaths of sweet incense, its
    measures of song,
And the light that is gilding its number-
    less towers?

See! forth from the gates, like a bridal
    array,
Come the princes of heaven, how
    bravely they shine!
'Tis to welcome the stranger, to show
    me the way,
And to tell me that all I see round me is
    mine.

There are millions of saints in their
    ranks and degrees,
And each with a beauty and crown of
    his own;
And there, far outnumbering the sands
    of the seas,
The nine rings of angels encircle the
    throne.

And oh! if the exiles of earth could but
    win,

One sight of the beauty of Jesus above,
From that hour they would cease to be
    able to sin,
And earth would be heaven; for heaven
    is love.

F. W. Faber
(1814–1863)

THE SETTING SUN

The heavens declare the glory of God. . . . In them He has set a tabernacle for the sun.
PSALM 19:1, 4

When I behold yon arch magnificent
Spanning the gorgeous West, the
    autumnal bed
Where the great Sun now hides his
    weary head,
With here and there a purple isle,
    that rent
From that huge cloud, their solid
    continent,
Seem floating in a sea of golden light,
A fire is kindled in my musing sprite,
And Fancy whispers: Such the glories
    lent

To this our mortal life; most glowing
    fair,
But built on clouds, and melting while
    we gaze.
Yet since those shadowy lights sure
    witness bear
Of One not seen, the undying Sun
    and source
Of good and fair, who wisely them
    surveys
Will use them well to cheer his heaven-
    ward course.

John Keble
(1792–1866)

Mourn Not the Vanished Years

*I have fought the good fight, I have finished
the race, I have kept the faith.*
2 Timothy 4:7

I mourn no more my vanished years;
Beneath a tender rain,
An April rain of smiles and tears,
My heart is young again.

The west winds blow, and singing low,
I hear the glad streams run;
The windows of my soul I throw
Wide open to the sun.

No longer forward, nor behind,
I look in hope and fear;

But grateful, take the good I find,
The best of now, and here.

I plow no more a desert land
For harvest, weed and tare;
The manna dropping from God's hand,
Rebukes my painful care.

I break my pilgrim staff, I lay
Aside the toiling oar;
The angel sought so far away,
I welcome at my door.

Enough that blessings undeserved,
Have marked my erring track;
That wheresoe'er my feet have swerved
His chastening turned me back.

That more and more a providence
Of love is understood,
Making the springs of time and sense,
Sweet with eternal good.

That all the jarring notes of life
Seem blending in a psalm,

And all the angels of its strife,
Slow rounding into calm.

And so the shadows fall apart,
And so the west winds play;
And all the windows of my heart
I open to this day.

JOHN G. WHITTIER
(1807–1892)

The Day Just Begun

While we do not look at the things
which are seen. . .
2 Corinthians 4:18

*S*urely the day is done!
'Tis set of sun!
Long fall the shadows from the snowy hills;
Not yet have waked the sleepy little rills;
But the soft air
Floods everywhere—
Although the day is done.

We know the day is done:
Our feet have run
Unresting in the path that duty made;
Treading on thorns, of danger not
      afraid;

And rest in sweet,
Though night hours fleet,
And day comes on.

The day of life is done!
And set the sun!
Eyes dim to fairer sights than earth can
    show:
Ears heedless, though entrancing music
    flow.
And marble brow,
Unwrinkled now;
Indeed! The day is done!
But is the day yet done?
And set the sun?
When seas of amber light transfuse
    the air,
The Paradisiacal flowers bloom
    everywhere!
O'er purple hills
The sunshine thrills,
Heaven's day is just begun!

ANONYMOUS

REMEMBERED JOY

In Your presence is fullness of joy; at Your right hand are pleasures forevermore.
PSALM 16:11

Don't grieve for me, for now, I'm
   free!
I follow the plan God laid for me.
I saw His face;
I heard His call.
I took His hand and left it all. . .
I could not stay another day,

To love, to laugh, to work or play;
Tasks left undone must stay that way.
And if my parting has left a void,
Then fill it with Remembered Joy.

A friendship shared, a laugh, a kiss. . .
Ah yes, these things I, too, shall miss.

My life's been full, I've savored much:
Good times, good friends, a loved one's
   touch.
Perhaps my time seemed all too brief—
Don't shorten yours with undue grief.
Be not burdened with tears of sorrow.
Enjoy the Sunshine of the 'morrow.

Anonymous

Glory Beyond Words

Yours, O Lord, is the greatness,
the power and the glory.
1 Chronicles 29:11

The apostle Paul often became speechless when trying to express the grand rapture of his soul. At least nine times, in the book of Romans, he throws up his hands in his helpless search for proper words. The grace and glory of the Lord are so apparent to him as he thinks on the great plan of God for the Church, the Body of Christ, that he exclaims, "What shall we say then?!" Many mere mortals have tried in vain to rise to the task. All are speechless. The words must yet be created.

God knows His redeemed ones long to be able to thank Him for His goodness and mercy. It is He, through His Holy Spirit, who reveals His glory to mankind. He created the minds of men. He prepared the first dictionary of words, for universal understanding of His own thoughts. He gave His thoughts to man in His holy Word. But where are there adequate words to express man's praise?

Take all the Psalms of David. They are many, and they are marvelous, yet they too fall short of giving the glory due to the all-worthy name of our Lord and Savior, Jesus Christ. Take all the expressions of other writers of Holy Scripture. They do not satisfy the longings of the redeemed to praise Him. Many writers and noble poets have tried to find adequate words:

> O worship the King, all glorious above
>   and gratefully sing His wonderful
>   love.
> Our Shield and Defender, the Ancient
>   of Days, pavillioned in splendor and
>   girded with praise.
> O tell of His might and sing of His
>   grace

Whose robe is the light, whose canopy,
    space.
His chariots of wrath the deep thunder
    clouds form
And dark is His path on the wings of
    the storm.

Thy bountiful care, what tongue can
    recite
It breathes in the air, it shines in the
    light.
It streams from the hills, it descends to
    the plain
And sweetly distills in the dew and the
    rain.

Sir Robert Grant

There is more to say. In eternity we shall find those words. George Frederic Handel wrote the "Messiah" after carefully and prayerfully studying the Scriptures given to him by his friend, Charles Jennens. The great choruses of praise and adoration lift the heart to the very realms of glory: "The Glory of the Lord," "The People Have Seen a Great

Light," "Glory to God," "Rejoice Greatly," "Lift Up Your Heads Oh Ye Gates," "The Hallelujah Chorus," "The Trumpet Shall Sound," and "Worthy Is the Lamb" rise in ever-increasing declaration of praise to Him who alone is worthy. Handel's magnificent conclusion was the "Amen" where all the parts burst forth in repeated turns, enhanced by music sublime. Again and again the "Amen" is sung. One could almost "see" all the mighty angelic realm, all the heavenly beings rapturously voicing praise. "Worthy is the lamb that was slain to receive power and riches, wisdom and strength, and honor and glory and blessing."

We earthlings, the Redeemed, join Handel and the hosts of heaven and earth exclaiming, "Thine, Oh Lord, is the greatness, and the power, and the glory."

Amen.

JOY HALEY BROWN

SUNSET AND EVENING STAR

As for me,
I will see Your face in righteousness;
I shall be satisfied when I awake
in Your likeness.
PSALM 17:15

*S*unset and evening star.
And one clear call for me!
And may there be no moaning of the
bar,
When I put out to sea,

But such a tide as moving seems asleep,
Too full for sound and foam,
When that which drew from out the
boundless deep
Turns again home.

Twilight and evening bell,
And after that the dark!
And may there be no sadness of
　　farewell,
When I embark;

For though from out our bourne of
　　Time and Place
The flood may bear me far,
I hope to see my Pilot face to face
When I have crossed the bar.

ALFRED, LORD TENNYSON
(1809–1892)

ON THE "ELEGY WRITTEN IN A COUNTRY CHURCHYARD"

For to me, to live is Christ, and to die is gain.
PHILIPPIANS 1:21

The "Elegy" was first published in 1751. Thomas Gray almost certainly took as the model for his poem the church and yard of St. Giles at Stoke Poges in Buckinghamshire, England. The poem's success was instantaneous and overwhelming, and it quickly ran through eleven editions.

Dr. Samuel Johnson said that "it abounds with images that find a mirror in every mind," and Tennyson, a century later, spoke of its "divine truisms." James Boswell, Johnson's famous biographer, was not alone in looking to the lines of Thomas Gray as a model for his own spiritual deportment in the face of adversity, and "stoically reminded himself in his own diary to buckle down and 'Be Gray.' " The submissive and grateful acceptance of our own particular destinies in our earthly pilgrimage is for each of us a priority task.

General James Wolfe on the memorable night preceding the taking of Quebec on September 13, 1759, is said to have repeated the entire elegy. Upon concluding the recitation, he said to his companions in arms, "Now, gentlemen, I would prefer being the author of that poem to the glory of beating the French tomorrow."

Daniel Webster (1782–1852), the American statesman, was heard to repeat during a severe illness, somewhat indistinctly, "Poet, poetry—Gray, Gray." His son repeated the first line of the "Elegy"—"The curfew tolls the knell of parting day"—"That's it! That's it!" exclaimed Mr. Webster. The book was brought, and other stanzas read, which provided for the great man of God a heartening cordial.

THE ELEGY

The curfew tolls the knell of parting
day,
The lowing herds wind slowly o'er the
lea,
The plowman homeward plods his
weary way,
And leaves the world to darkness and
to me.

Now fades the glimmering landscape on
the sight,
And all the air a solemn stillness holds,
Save where the beetle wheels his dron-
ing flight,
And drowsy tinklings lull the distant
folds;

Save that from yonder ivy-mantled
      tower,
The moping owl does to the moon
      complain
Of such as, wandering near her secret
      bower,
Molest her ancient solitary reign.

Beneath those rugged elms, that yew-
      tree's shade,
Where heaves the turf in many a
      moldering heap,
Each in his narrow cell forever laid,
The rude forefathers of the hamlet
      sleep.

The breezy call of incense-breathing
      morn,
The swallow twittering from the straw-
      built shed,
The cock's shrill clarion, or the echoing
      horn.
No more shall rouse them from their
      lowly bed.

For them no more the blazing hearth
    shall burn,
Or busy housewife ply her evening
    care:
No children run to lisp their sire's
    return,
Or climb his knees the envied kiss to
    share.

Oft did the harvest to their sickle yield,
Their furrow oft the stubborn glebe has
    broke;
How jocund did they drive their team
    afield!
How bowed the woods beneath their
    sturdy stroke!

Let not Ambition mock their useful toil,
Their homely joys, and destiny obscure;
Nor Grandeur hear with a disdainful
    smile
The short and simple annals of the poor.

The boast of heraldry, the pomp of
    power,

And all that beauty, all that wealth e'er
    gave,
Await alike the inevitable hour:
The paths of glory lead but to the grave.

Nor you, ye proud, impute to these the
    fault,
If Memory o'er their tomb be trophies
    raise,
Where through the long-drawn aisle
    and fretted vault
The pealing anthem swells the note of
    praise.

Can storied urn or animated bust
Back to its mansion call the fleeting
    breath?
Can Honor's voice provoke the silent
    dust,
Or Flattery soothe the dull cold ear of
    Death?

Perhaps in this neglected spot is laid
Some heart once pregnant with celestial
    fire;

Hands that the rod of empire might
    have swayed,
Or waked to ecstasy the living lyre.

But knowledge to their eyes her ample
    page
Rich with the spoils of time did ne'er
    unroll;
Chill Penury repressed their noble rage,
And froze the genial current of the soul.

Full many a gem of purest ray serene,
The dark unfathomed caves of ocean
    bear:
Full many a flower is born to blush
    unseen,
And waste its sweetness on the desert air.

Some village Hampden, that with
    dauntless breast
The little tyrant of his fields withstood;
Some mute inglorious Milton here may
    rest,
Some Cromwell guiltless of his country's
    blood.

The applause of listening senates to
    command,
The threats of pain and ruin to despise,
To scatter plenty o'er a smiling land,
And read their history in a nation's eyes.

Their lot forbade; nor circumscribed
    alone
Their glowing virtues, but their crimes
    confined;
Forbade to wade through slaughter to a
    throne,
And shut the gates of mercy on
    mankind;

The struggling pangs of conscious truth
    to hide,
To quench the blushes of ingenuous
    shame,
Or heap the shrine of Luxury and Pride
With incense kindled at the Muse's
    flame.

Far from the madding crowd's ignoble
    strife

Their sober wishes never learned to
    stray;
Along the cool sequestered vale of life
They kept the noiseless tenor of their
    way.

Yet e'en these bones from insult to
    protect,
Some frail memorial still erected nigh,
With uncouth rhymes and shapeless
    sculpture decked,
Implores the passing tribute of a sigh.

Their name, their years, spelt by the
    unlettered muse,
The place of fame and elegy supply.
And many a holy text around she
    strews,
That teach the rustic moralist to die.

For who, to dumb Forgetfulness a prey,
This pleasing anxious being e'er
    resigned,
Left the warm precincts of the cheerful
    day,

Nor cast one longing, lingering look
    behind?

On some fond breast the parting soul
    relies,
Some pious drops the closing eye
    requires;
Even from the tomb the voice of nature
    cries,
Even in our ashes live their wonted fires.

For thee, who mindful of the
    unhonored dead,
Dost in these lines their artless tale
    relate;
If chance, by lonely Contemplation led,
Some kindred spirit shall inquire thy
    fate;

Haply some hoary-headed swain may
    say,
"Oft have we seen him at the peep of
    dawn
Brushing with hasty steps the dews
    away,

To meet the sun upon the upland lawn.

"There at the foot of yonder nodding
    beech,
That wreathes its old fantastic roots so
    high,
His listless length at noontide would he
    stretch,
And pore upon the brook that babbles by.

"Hard by yon wood, now smiling as in
    scorn,
Muttering his wayward fancies he would
    rove;
Now drooping, woeful, wan, like one
    forlorn,
Or crazed with care, or crossed in hope-
    less love.

"One morn I missed him on the 'cus-
    tomed hill,
Along the heath and near his favorite
    tree;
Another came; nor yet beside the rill,

Nor up the lawn, nor at the wood
    was he:

"The next, with dirges due in sad array
Slow through the church-way path we
    see him borne:
Approach and read (for thou canst read)
    the lay
Graved on the stone beneath yon aged
    thorn."

The Epitaph

Here rests his head upon the lap of
    Earth,
A Youth, to Fortune and to Fame
    unknown;
Fair Science frowned not on his humble
    birth,
And Melancholy marked him for her
    own.

Large was his bounty, and his soul
    sincere,
Heaven did a recompense as largely
    send:
He gave to Misery all he had, a tear,
He gained from Heaven ('twas all he
    wished) a friend.

No farther seek his merits to disclose,
Or draw his frailties from their dread
　　abode,
(There they alike in trembling hope
　　repose),
The bosom of his Father and his God.

THOMAS GRAY
(1716–1771)

ACKNOWLEDGMENTS

Barbour Publishing, Inc., expresses its appreciation to all those who generously gave permission to reprint and/or adapt copyrighted material. Diligent effort has been made to identify, locate, and contact copyright holders, and to secure permission to use copyrighted material. If any permissions or acknowledgments have been inadvertently omitted or if such permissions were not received by the time of publication, the publisher would sincerely appreciate receiving complete information so that correct credit can be given in future editions.

1. "Until Then," written by Stuart Hamblen, Hamblen Music (ASCAP), copyright 1958, renewed 1986. Used by permission. All rights reserved.

2. Viteslav Gardavsky, "God Is Not Yet Dead," quoted in Eugene H. Peterson, *Run with the Horses* (Downers Grove, Ill.: InterVarsity, 1983), 17.

3. Fred Smith, "Making Your Message Memorable," *Leadership* (Spring 1998): 94.

4. Excerpted from *Bibliotheca Sacra,* Vol. 157, by Dr. Howard G. Hendricks. Used by permission.

5. "I Have Only Begun to Live," by Richard W. DeHaan, *Our Daily Bread,* copyright 1987 by RBC Ministries, Grand Rapids, MI. Reprinted by permission.

6. "The Path I Have Prepared for You," by Roy Lessin, reprinted by permission of the author.

7. "Think Through Me Thoughts of God," by Amy Carmichael, from *Learning of God,* published by Christian Literature Crusade. Used by permission.

8. "Re-Ignited," by Haddon Robinson, reprinted by permission of the author.